SWU-NAP- 006

UNIFORMS OF RUSSIAN ARMY DURING THE NAPOLEONIC WAR VOL.1

UNDER THE REIGN OF PAUL I
EMPEROR OF RUSSIA BETWEEN 1796 AND 1801
INFANTRY FUSILIERS, GRENADIERS & MUSKETEERS

From the Viskovatov's greatest work:
"Historical description of the clothing and
arms of the Russian Army"

English translation by Mark Conrad

SOLDIERSHOP PUBLISHING

AUTHOR

Aleksandr Vasilevich Viskovatov born 22 April (4 May New Style) 1804, died 27 February (11 March) 1858 in St. Petersburg, Russian military historian. He graduated from the 1st Cadet Corps and served in the artillery, the hydrographic depot of the Naval Ministry, and then in the Department of Military Educational Institutions. He mainly studied historical artifacts and the histories of military units. Viskovatov's greatest work was the Historical Description of the Clothing and Arms of the Russian Army.

TRANSLATOR

Mark Conrad is an American historian with a great interest for all the Russian history.

Title: **UNIFORMS OF RUSSIAN ARMY DURING THE NAPOLEONIC WAR VOL. 1 -**
The Infantry Fusiliers, Grenadiers and Musketeers
By A.V.Viskovatov. English translation by Mark Conrad. First edition by Soldiershop.
Cover & Art Design: Luca S. Cristini. Plates re-colorations by Anna Cristini
ISBN code: 978-88-93270472

Published by Soldiershop publishing, via Padre Davide, 7 - 24050 Zanica (BG) ITALY. www.soldiershop.com

UNIFORMS
OF THE RUSSIAN
ARMY DURING THE
NAPOLEONIC WAR VOL.1

UNDER THE REIGN OF PAUL I EMPEROR OF
RUSSIA BETWEEN 1796 AND 1801

*

The Infantry Fusiliers, Grenadiers and Musketeers

Сост. и рис. Пиратский.   Лит. Главн. упр. Путей Сообщенія и Публич. зданій. (Дир. К. Поль)   Рисна кам. Шинд

1800 ГОДА.

Л. Гв. Измайловскій полкъ въ годъ назначенія Его Императорскаго Высочества
Великаго Князя Николая Павловича Шефомъ сего полка.

HISTORICAL DESCRIPTION OF THE CLOTHING AND ARMS
OF THE RUSSIAN ARMY - A.V. VISKOVATOV
(First English translation by Mark Conrad)

Soldiershop is glad to presents the complete collection of the great job made by A.V. Viskovatov dedicated to the uniforms and weapons belonging to the Russian army during the Napoleonic period, until 1825. The time we considered corresponds to the reigns of two Tzars: Paul I, who reigned since 1769 until his murder on the 23rd of March 1801, and his son Aleksandr Pavlovi☐ Romanov, that with the title of Alexander I, sat on the throne until the 1st December 1825.

Our reprint in based on the original 19th century volumes, to be precise the volumes from 7 to 9 are dedicated to the reign of Paul I; this first part is distributed on 7 volumes, having a numbering from 1 to 7. From number 10 to 18 of the original volumes, the second part is dedicated to the Russian troops under Alexander I. These still being worked on and they will be soon ready, distributed on twenty volumes approximately. Our new edition, the first ever published in English, both on paper and digital format, boasts a large number of color plates, many of them unpublished and coloured by our team of expert artists and scholars of uniformology. Each volume is based on 50/70 plates, always accompanied by the original translated text which describes the uniforms, the organization and the armament of the Russian army of the period.

A unique work in its genre, a must have in any respecting collection!

Aleksandr Vasilevich Viskovatov born 22 April (4 May New Style) 1804, died 27 February (11 March) 1858 in St. Petersburg, Russian military historian. He graduated from the 1st Cadet Corps and served in the artillery, the hydrographic depot of the Naval Ministry, and then in the Department of Military Educational Institutions.

He mainly studied historical artifacts and the histories of military units. Viskovatov's greatest work was the Historical Description of the Clothing and Arms of the Russian Army (Vols. 1-30, St. Petersburg, 1841-62; 2nd ed. Vols. 1-34, St. Petersburg - Novosibirsk - Leningrad, 1899-1948). This work is based on a great quantity of archival documents and contains four thousand colored illustrations.

Viskovatov was the author of Chronicles of the Russian Army (Books 1-20, St. Petersburg, 1834-42) and Chronicles of the Russian Imperial Army (Parts 1-7, St. Petersburg, 1852). He collected valuable material on the history of the Russian navy which went into A Short Overview of Russian Naval Campaigns and General Voyages to the End of the XVII Century (St. Petersburg, 1864; 2nd edition Moscow, 1946). Together with A.I. Mikhailovskii-Danilevskii he helped prepare and create the Military Gallery in the Winter Palace.

He wrote the historical military inscriptions for the walls of the Hall of St. George in the Great Palace of the Kremlin. (From the article in the Soviet Military Encyclopedia.)

CONTENTS

*

Preface pag. 5

*

Russian Army organization pag. 7

*

Notes pag. 38

*

Plates pag. 43

RUSSIAN ARMY
ORGANIZATION 1796-1801

Military Land Forces on 6 November 1796 :

I.   Field Infantry.
II.   Cavalry.
III.   Artillery.
IV.   Corps of Engineers.
V.   Garrisons.
VI.   Guards Infantry.
VII.   Guards Cavalry.
VIII.   Guards Artillery.
IX.   Military Educational Establishments.
X.   Cossack forces.
XI.   National forces.
XII.   Temporary forces.
XIII.   Special commands at various official places and government buildings, and other separate units of the military administration.
XIV.   State companies and commands.
XV.   Non-serving invalids.
XVI.   Marine troops.

Changes in the composition and nomenclature of all forces, from 1796 to 1801

Upon Emperor Paul I's ascension to the Throne on 6 November 1796, Russian forces were as follows:

I. **Cavalier Guards Corps** (*Kavelergardskii Korpus*).
II. *Life-Guards* regiments: **Preobrazhenskii, Semenovskii, Izmailovskii**, and **Horse** (*Konnyi*).
III. At the Imperial court (*Sostoyavshie pri VYSOCHAISOCHAISHEMDVORE*): **Leib-Hussar Squadron** (*Leib Gusarskii eskadron*) and **cossack escort commands** (*konvoinyya kazach'i komandy*): **Chuguev** and **Don**.
IV. *Grenadier* regiments: Leib-Grenadiers, Taurica (*Tavricheskii*), Yekaterinoslav, Little-Russia (*Malorossiiskii*), Kiev, Siberia, Phanagoria, Astrakhan, St.-Petersburg, Kherson, Moscow (*Moskovskii*), and Caucasus.
V. *Infantry or musketeer* regiments: Old-Ingermanland (*Staroingermanlandskii*), Moscow (*Moskovskii*), Troitsk, Vladimir, Novgorod, Schlüsselburg, Kazan, Pskov, Smolensk, Azov, Voronezh, Nizhnii-Novgorod (*Nizhegorodskii*), Chernigov, Ryazan, Suzdal, Rostov, Velikie-Luki (*Velikolutskii*), Archangel (*Arkhangelogorodskii*), Perm, Vyatka, Narva, Tobolsk, Neva, Vitebsk, Viborg,

Uglich, Kexholm, Ladoga, Belozersk, Murom, Apsheron, Shirvan, Kabarda, Nasheburg, Nizovsk, Tiflis, Staryi-Oskol (*Staroskol'sk*), Belev, Ryazhsk, Sevsk, Yelets, Tambov, Orel (*Orlovskii*), Bryansk, Kursk, Kozlov, Aleksopol, Reval, Polotsk, Dnieper, Tula, Sevastopol, Sofiya, New-Ingermanland (*Novoingermanlandskii*), and Yaroslavl. In addition there were planned to be formed: Voznesensk, Bratslav, Podolia, Volhynia (*Volynskii*), Courland (*Kurlyandskii*), Tiraspol, Odessa, Minsk, Vilna, and Kovno (*Kovenskii*).

VI. *Field* battalions (*Polevye bataliony*): Yekaterinburg, Semipalatinsk; 3rd, 4th, 5th, and 6th Siberia; 1st, 2nd, 3rd, 4th, 5th, and 6th Orenburg; 1st, 2nd, 3rd, 4th, 5th, 6th, 7th, and 8th Moscow.

VII. *Jäger* regiments (*Yegerskie polki*): **Kuban**, **Caucasus**, **Taurica**, **Bug**, **Belorussia**, **Finland**, **Livonia** (*Liflyandskii*), **Yekaterinoslav**, **Estonia** (*Estlyandskii*), and **Lithuania** (*Litovskii*).

VIII. *Jäger* battalions: **1st** and **2nd Siberia** and the **Olonets**.

IX. *Cuirassier* regiments (*Kirasirskie polki*): **Leib-Cuirassiers, the Heir's** (*Naslednika*), **Military Order** (*Voennago Ordena*), **Kazan**, and **Prince Potemkin's** (*Knayz' Potemkina*).

X. *Carabineer* regiments (*Karabinernye polki*): Riga(*Rizhskii*), Narva, Ryazan, Kargopol, Rostov, Moscow, Yamburg, Ingermanland, Sofiya, Glukhov, Tver, Kiev, Seversk, Chernigov, Nezhin, and Starodub.

XI. **Military Order Horse-GrenadierRegiment** (Konno-Grenaderskii polk Voennago Ordena).

XII. *Dragoon* regiments: Astrakhan, Vladimir, Smolensk, Taganrog, Kinburn, Nizhnii-Novgorod (*Nizhegorodskii*), St.-Petersburg, Orenburg, Siberia, Irkutsk, and Voronezh.

XIII. *Hussar* regiments: **Olviopol** and **Voronezh**, 5 hussar squadrons with the **Pskov Dragoon Regiment** and 2 squadrons with the **Moscow Police.**

XIV. *Light-Horse* regiments (*Legko-konnye polki*): Mariupol, Pavlograd, Aleksandriya, Kherson, Poltava, Ostrorog, Akhtyrka, Sumy, Kharkov, Izyum, and Ukraine.

XV. *Horse-Jäger* regiments: **Pereyaslavl**, **Yelisavetgrad**, **Kiev**, and **Taurica**.

XVI. Regiments of the *Foot Field Artillery*: **Bombardier**, **1st** and **2nd Cannoneer**, and **1st** and **2nd Fusilier**; 3 battalions: **1st, 2nd,** and **3rd Bombardier**.

XVII *Horse Artillery*: of **5 companies.**

XVIII. 3 companies of *engineers*: **Miner Company**, **Pioneer Company**, and **Engineer Company for the Southern Borders** (*Minernaya, Pionernaya i Inzhenernaya dlya yuzhnykh granits*).

XIX. *Garrison* battalions: 1st, 2nd, 3rd, 4th, and 5th St.-Petersburg; 1st, 2nd, and 3rd Kronstadt; 1st and 2nd Narva; 1st, 2nd, 3rd, and 4th Viborg; 1st and 2nd Fredrikshamn; Nyslott; Villmanstrand; Kexholm; 1st, 2nd, 3rd, and 4th Reval; Dünamünde; Pernau; Arensburg; 1st and 2nd Smolensk; Rogerviks; Dünaburg; 1st, 2nd, 3rd, and 4th Riga; Polotsk; Vitebsk; Senno (*Sennenskii*); Rogachev; Staryi-Bykhov; 1st and 2nd Kiev; 1st, 2nd, and 3rd St.-Elizabeth Fortress (*kreposti Sv. Yelisavety*); 1st, 2nd, and 3rd St.-Dimitrii Fortress (*kreposti Sv. Dimitriya*); Bakhmut; 1st and 2nd Azov; 1st, 2nd, and 3rd Taganrog; Tambov; Kirillov; Aleksandrovsk; Petrovsk; Nikitinsk and Dneprovsk; 1st, 2nd, 3rd, and 4th Astrakhan; 1st and 2nd Tsaritsyn; Saratov; 1st and 2nd Kizlyar; Mozdok; 1st, 2nd, and 3rd Tobolsk; Tomsk; 1st and 2nd Omsk; Semipalatinsk; Biisk; St.-Peter Fortress (*kresposti Sv. Petra*); Irkutsk; 1st and 2nd Selenginsk; 1st, 2nd, 3rd, and 4th Orenburg; Ozernaya; Kizilsk; Verkhne-Uralsk; Troitsk; Zverinogolovsk; Stavropol; Novgorod; Tver; 1st, 2nd, and 3rd Moscow; Vladimir; Perekop; 1st, 2nd, and 3rd Kazan; Nizhnii-Novgorod; Simbirsk; 1st and 2nd Archangel; Voronezh.

XX. Cadet corps: **IMPERIAL Land, Artillery, and Engineer** (Imperatorskii Sukhoputnyi, Artilleriiskii i Inzhenernyi); **Foreign Co-Believers** (Chuzestrannykh yedinovertsev).

XXI. *Cossack* hosts: **Don, Black-Sea, Siberian, Orenburg, Astrakhan,** and **Yekaterinoslav.** Cossack regiments on a regular establishment: **1st, 2nd,** and **3rd Chuguev; Astrakhan, Mozdok; 1st, 2nd,** and **3rd Orenburg; Ufa.** Settled Caucasian cossacks: **Grebensk, Terek, Family** (*Semeinye*), **Khoper,** and **Volga; Stavropol baptized Kalmyks.**

XXII. *National forces:* Mozdok Mountaineer Command (*Gorskaya Mozdokskaya komanda*); Greek Infantry Regiment; IMPERIAL Belorussian, Mogilev, and Polotsk Standards (*Khorugvi*); Tauric Tatar double-squadrons (*diviziony*) (two in number); Greek double-squadron (near Odessa).

XXIII. Temporary forces formed under special military circumstances: **Corps of Little-Russian Foot Riflemen** (Korpus Malorossiiskikh peshikh strelkov) and a **Cossack regiment of wagon drivers** (Kazachii polk iz yamshchikov).

XXIV. *Detachments at official places and government institutions,* such as: at the **Senate**-a battalion; at the **Main War Commissariat** and on the **Provisioning establishment**-one company each; at the **St.-Petersburg Educational Society for Noble-Born Girls,** at the **Main Salt Office** and its branches, at the construction of the **Moscow Kremlin palace,** at the **St.-Petersburg Nobles' Bank,** at the **Troitsk Commerce Office,** at the **Main Court Chancellery,** at the **Collegium for Foreign Affairs,** at the **Patrimonial Estates Department** (*Votchinnyi Departament*), and at the **foundry in the Donets District**-one detachment (*komanda*) each.

XXV. *Mines* battalions: Kolyvan-Voskresensk and Nerchinsk battalions. Companies: at the Yekaterinburg gold works-two infantry; at the Goroblagodatsk and Kamsk mines-one infantry; at the Olonets Petrovsk works-one invalid.

XXVI. *State Commands (Shtatnyya Komandy):* in St.-Petersburg Province-10, Arkhangel Province-7, Olonets Province-8, Viborg Province-6, Reval Province-5, Riga Province-9, Pskov Province-9, Vologda Province-12, B-12, Kostroma Province-15, Vyatka Province-13, Perm Province-15, Tobolsk Province-16, Moscow Province-15, Smolensk Province-12, Polotsk Province-11, Mogilev Province-12, Chernigov Province-15, Novgorod-Severskii Province-11, Kharkov Province-15, Kursk Province-15, Orel Province-13, Kaluga Province-12, Tula Province-12, Ryazan Province-2, Vladimir Province-14, Nizhnii-Novgorod Province-13, Kazan Province-13, Simbirsk Province-13, Penza Province-13, Tambov Province-12, Voronezh Province-15, Saratov Province-11, Ufa Province-13, Kolyvan Province-5, Irkutsk Province-4, Kiev Province-10, Yekaterinoslav Province-15, Taurica Region-7, Caucasus Province-9, and Courland Province-9.

XXVII. *Non-Serving Invalid Commands (Komandy nesluzhashchikh Invalidov):* Life-Guards, Murom, Khlynsk, Kasimovsk, Arzamas, Shatsk, Tambov, Penza, Lebedyansk, Kozmodemyansk, Cheboksary, Kadomsk, Alatyrsk, Temnikovsk, Kerensk, Saransk, Nizhne-Lomovsk, Insarsk, Putivl, Pronsk, Kozelsk, Ryazhsk, Bezhetsk, Zaraisk, Syzransk, Urzhumsk, Yadrinsk, Kurmyshsk, Slobodsk, Kozlov, Sviyazh, and Verkhne-Lomovsk.

XXVIII. *Naval troops under the command of the War Collegium:* Baltic Fleet-**1st** and **2nd Marine Regiments** and **1st** and **2nd Bombardier Battalions**; Black-Sea Fleet-**Grenadier Corps** and **Bombardier Battalion.**

Apart for these forces, there were various military personnel in the **field artillery supply train** (*Polevoi Artilleriiskii Furshtat*), **arsenals**, **laboratories**, **powder works**, and **Engineer administration**.

The troops of the Heir, Grand Duke PAUL PETROVICH, the so-called *Gatchina troops*, consisted of: battalions-the Heir's (*Naslednika*), **Grand Duke ALEXANDER PAVLOVICH'S**, **Grand Duke CONSTANTINE PAVLOVICH'S**, Colonel Arakcheev's, Major Malyutin's, and Major Nedobrov's; **Jäger Company**; **Cuirassier** or **Gendarme Regiment**, **Dragoon Regiment**, **Hussar Regiment**, **Cossack Regiment**, and **Artillery Company**.

In the composition and naming of all these forces, during the Reign of EMPEROR PAUL I there took place the following changes:

I. FIELD INFANTRY (*Polevaya Pekhota*)

7 November 1796 – The plan of 1795 to form **ten Infantry regiments** (Voznesensk, Bratslav, Podolia, Volhynia, Courland, Tiraspol, Odessa, Minsk, Vilna, and Kovno) is cancelled [1].

19 November 1796 – Half of the Moscow Grenadier Regiment is detached and titled **Major General Vadkovskii's Grenadier Regiment** [2].

22 November 1796 – This regiment is named the Pavlovsk Grenadier Regiment [3].

27 November 1796 – **Arakcheev's Musketeer Regiment** is formed from personnel from the St.-Petersburg Garrison battalions [4].

29 November 1796 – The several Jäger corps are broken up into separate **Jäger battalions**, and **six Musketeer regiments** are formed from Field battalions, after which the Field Infantry was prescribed to consist of the following 13 Grenadier regiments, 62 Musketeer regiments, and 20 Jäger battalions:

a.) *Grenadier regiments*-Leib-Grenadier, Pavlovsk, Yekaterinoslav, St.-Petersburg, Astrakhan, Kiev, Moscow, Little Russia, Siberia, Phanagoria, Kherson, Taurica, and Caucasus.

b.) *Musketeer regiments*-Belozersk, Nasheburg, Chernigov, New Ingermanland, Yaroslavl, Apsheron, Smolensk, Ryazhsk, Kursk, Kozlov, Sevastopol, Belev, Aleksopol, Shlüsselburg, Bryansk, Troitsk, Ladoga, Polotsk, Archangel, Old Ingermanland, Novgorod, Nizhnii-Novgorod, Vitebsk, Azov, Orel, Reval, Tula, Yelets, Pskov, Tambov, Rostov, Murom, Staryi-Oskol, Tobolsk, Tiflis, Voronezh, Kazan, Moscow, Kabarda, Vladimir, Uglich, Sevsk, Narva, Dnieper, Vyatka, Suzdal, Kexholm, Viborg, Ryazan, Neva, Velikii-Luki, Ufa, Rylsk (the last three being from Orenburg Field battalions), Yekaterinburg, Selenginsk, Tomsk (all three being from former Siberia Field battalions), and Arkharov's.

c.) *Jäger battalions:* from No. 1 through 20 inclusive.

Each Grenadier and each Musketeer regiment consisted of two battalions, of which a Grenadier battalion was of six Grenadier companies and a Musketeer battalion-of one Grenadier company and five Musketeer companies. A Jäger battalion consisted of five Jäger companies. In Grenadier battalions, one company was named a Flank company (*Fligel-rota*), so that there were two in each regiment [5].

3 December 1796 – All the above regiments and battalions were allotted among **twelve divisions** named after the inspectorates, into which divisions were also included Regular Cavalry regiments and some Garrisons [6]. The distribution to divisions was as follows:

1.) *St.-Petersburg Division* – Leib and Pavlovsk Grenadiers; Kexholm, Belozersk, Yeletsk, and Arkharov's Musketeers.

2.) *Moscow Division* – Astrakhan Grenadiers; Old Ingermanland, Viborg, Shlüsselburg, Yaroslavl, Nacheburg, Baden the Elder's (*Staro-Badenskii*) (renamed from the Kozlov), and Ryazhsk Musketeers.

3.) *Livonia (Liflyandskaya) Division* – St.-Petersburg and Taurica Grenadiers; Rostov, Nizovsk, Kursk, Smolensk, Perm, Polotsk, and Voronezh Musketeers.

4.) *Smolensk Division* – Moscow and Phanagoria Grenadiers; Rostov, Nizovsk, Kursk, Smolensk, Perm, Polotsk, and Voronezh Musketeers.

5.) *Lithuania (Litovskaya) Division* – Yekaterinoslav Grenadiers; Apsheron, Tambov, Murom, Tula, Pskov, and Staryi-Oskol Musketeers; 4th, 5th, 6th, 7th, and 8th Jäger Battalions.

6.) *Finland Division* – Ryazan Grenadiers; Velikie-Luki and Neva Musketeers, 1st, 2nd, and 3rd Jäger Battalions.

7.) *Ukraine Division* – Little-Russia and Kiev Grenadiers; Uglich, Vladimir, Moscow, New Ingermanland, Archangel, Narva, Bryansk, and Baden the Younger's (*Molodo-Badenskii*) (renamed from the Butyrsk) Musketeers.

8.) *Yekaterinoslav Division* - Siberia and Kherson Grenadiers; Azov, Orel, Novgorod, Nizhnii-Novgorod, Vyatka, Aleksopol, and Ladoga Mukseteers; 9th, 10th, 11th, 12th, 13th, and 14th Jäger Battalions.

9.) *Taurica Division* (later named the *Crimea Division*) – Sevastopol, Vitebsk, Troitsk, and Belev Musketeers; 15th and 16th Jäger Battalions.

10.) *Caucasus Division* – Caucasus Grenadiers; Kabarda, Kazan, Suzdal, and Tiflis Musketeers; 17th and 18th Jäger Battalions.

11.) *Orenburg Division*– Rylsk, Ufa, and Yekaterinoslav Musketeers.

12.) *Siberia Division* – Shirvan, Tomsk, and Selenginsk Musketeers; 19th and 20th Jäger Battalions.

13 December 1796 – Flank companies in Grenadier regiments and grenadier companies in Musketeer regiments are ordered to form *Combined Grenadier battalions (Svodnye Grenadirskie bataliony)*, which were named after the field-grade officers commanding them. They were formed from companies of the following regiments:

1.) St.-Petersburg Division:
From companies of the Kexholm Musketeers and Arkharov's Musketeer Regiment
    ”   ”   ” Pavlovsk Grenadiers and Belozersk Musketeers
    ”   ”   ” Yelets Musketeers and Ryazan Musketeers

2.) Moscow Division:
From companies of the Old-Ingermanland Musketeers and Ryazhsk Musketeers
    ”   ”   ” Kozlov Musketeers and Shlüsselburg Musketeers
    ”   ”   ” Astrakhan Grenadiers and Yaroslavl Musketeers
    ”   ”   ” Viborg Musketeers and Nasheburg Musketeers

3.) Livonia Division:
From companies of the St.-Petersburg Grenadiers and Taurica Grenadiers
    ”   ”   ” Dnieper Musketeers and Tobolsk Musketeers
    ”   ”   ” Reval Musketeers and Sevsk Musketeers
    ”   ”   ” Sofiya Musketeers and Chernigov Musketeers

4.) Smolensk Division:

From companies of the Rostov Musketeers and Nizovsk Musketeers
       "   "   "   Smolensk Musketeers and Kursk Musketeers
       "   "   "   Polotsk Musketeers and Voronezh Musketeers
       "   "   "   Moscow Grenadiers and Yekaterinoslav Grenadiers

5.) Lithuania Division:

From companies of the Apsheron Musketeers and Murom Musketeers
       "   "   "   Tambov Musketeers and Tula Musketeers
       "   "   "   Polotsk Musketeers and Voronezh Musketeers
       "   "   "   Stavropol Musketeers and Pskov Musketeers

6.) Finland Division:

From companies of the Velikie-Luki Musketeers and Neva Musketeers

7.) Ukraine Division:

From companies of the Little-Russia Grenadiers and Kiev Grenadiers
       "   "   "   Vladimir Musketeers and New-Ingermanland Musketeers
       "   "   "   Butyrsk Musketeers and Bryansk Musketeers
       "   "   "   Narva Musketeers and Moscow Musketeers
       "   "   "   Uglich Musketeers and Archangel Musketeers

8.) Yekaterinoslav Division:

From companies of the Siberia Grenadiers and Kherson Grenadiers
       "   "   "   Azov Musketeers and Orel Musketeers
       "   "   "   Novgorod Musketeers and Nizhnii-Novgorod Musketeers
       "   "   "   Vyatka Musketeers and Aleksopol Musketeers

9.) Taurica Division:

From companies of the Sevastopol Musketeers and Vitebsk Musketeers
       "   "   "   Troitsk Musketeers and Belev Musketeers

10.) Caucasus Division:

From companies of the Suzdal Musketeers and Tiflis Musketeers
       "   "   "   Kazan Musketeers and Kabarda Musketeers

11.) Orenburg Division:

From companies of the Rylsk Musketeers and Ufa Musketeers(if !supportLineBreakNewLine)

12.) Siberia Division:

From companies of the Shirvan Musketeers and Tomsk Musketeers

This listing was made in accordance with the distribution of troop quarters and thus changed at various times during the rest of EMPEROR PAUL I's reign. In the Ladoga Musketeers, as well as the Caucasus Grenadiers and Yekaterinburg and Estonia Musketeers, companies were not detached to form combined battalions: the last three because their quarters were so far from other regiments and the first because in the Yekaterinoslav Division, to which it belonged, there was no other regiment left over for detaching companies [7].

16 January 1797 – The **Leib-Grenadier Regiment**, of two battalions, is reformed as four battalions, with each battalion to have five companies [8].

17 May 1797 – **Jäger battalions** are renamed as **regiments**, keeping their previous numbers and bringing them to a two-battalion organization, with each battalion to have five companies [9].

14 September 1797 – Arkharov's Musketeer Regiment is named *Maj.-Gen. Graf Elmpt's Musketeer Regiment* [10].

22 September 1797 – The Yekaterinoslav Division is named the *Dnieper Division* [11].

11 January 1798 – The Yekaterinoslav Grenadier Regiment is named the *Pskov Grenadier Regiment* [12].

20 August 1798 – New musketeer regiments, formed from recruits, are named after their chefs: Maj.-Gen. Pavlutskii's, Maj.-Gen. Leitner's, Maj.-Gen. Brant's, Maj.-Gen. Müller 1st's(Millera 1-go), Maj.-Gen. Marklovskii 1st's, and Maj.-Gen. von Berg's(fon-Berkha) [13].

2 October 1798 – The Kexholm, Yelets, and Belozersk Musketeer Regiments are named after their *chefs*: the first as *Maj.-Gen. Sukov's Musketeers*, the second as *Maj.-Gen. Vadkovskii's*, and the third as *Lt.-Gen. Budkevich's* [14].

18 October 1798 – The Old-Ingermanland Musketeer Regiment is named *Maj.-Gen. von Klugen's*, and *Maj.-Gen. Graf Elmpt's* (formerly Arkharov's) is named *Maj.-Gen. Ukolov's Musketeer Regiment* [15].

21 October 1798 – The last regiment above is named *Maj.-Gen. Graf Elmpt's Musketeers* for the second time, and the New Ingermanland as *Maj.-Gen. Baron Rosen's* (*Rozena*) Musketeers [16].

24 October 1798 – The Kiev Grenadier Regiment is named *Gen.-of-Inf. Bekleshov's Grenadier Regiment* [17].

26 October 1798 – The Vyatka Musketeer Reg. is named *Maj.-Gen. Samarin's Musketeer Regiment* [18].

31 October 1798 – All Grenadier (except the Leib-Grenadiers), Musketeer, and Jäger regiments are ordered to be named after their *Chefs*. Consequently, they received the following designations, with subsequent changes [19]:

Pavlovsk Grenadiers – from 31 October 1798 – *Maj.-Gen. Emme's Grenadiers*; 8 April 1800 – *Maj.-Gen. Kerbits'*.

Pskov Grenadiers (formerly Yekaterinoslav) – 31 October 1798 – *Lt.-Gen. Baron von der Osten-Sacken 1st's*; 24 October 1799 – *Maj.-Gen. Palitsyn's*.

St.-Petersburg Grenadiers – 31 October 1798 – Maj.-Gen. Prince Golitsyn 2nd's; 24 March 1800 – Maj.-Gen. Prince Volkonskii 3rd's; 3 May 1800 – Maj.-Gen. Safonov's; 2 January 1801 – Lt.-Gen. Baron fon der Osten-Sacken 1st's.

Astrakhan Grenadiers– 31 October 1798 – Maj.-Gen. Borozdin 1st's; 19 February 1799 – Lt.-Gen. the Crown Prince of Mecklenburg's.

Gen.-of-Inf. Bekleshov's Grenadiers (formerly Kiev) – 31 October 1798 – as previously, *Gen.-of-Inf. Bekleshov's*; 7 June 1799 – *Maj.-Gen. Passeck's* (*Passeka*).

Moscow Grenadiers – 31 October 1798 – Gen.-of-Inf. Rosenberg's (Rozenberga); 8 June 1800 – Maj.-Gen. Prince Carl of Mecklenberg's.

Little-Russia Grenadiers – 31 October 1798 – *Maj.Gen. Radt's*; 19 November 1800 – *Maj.Gen. Berg's*.

Siberia Grenadiers – 31 October 1798 – *Maj.-Gen. Lyapunov's*; 31 March 1800 – *Maj. Gen. Bakhmetev 3rd's*.

Phanagoria Grenadiers – 31 October 1798 – *Maj.-Gen. Zherebtsov's*; 27 September 1799 – *Maj.-Gen. Mamaev's*.

Kherson Grenadiers – 31 October 1798 – *Lt.Gen. Galberg's*; 6 November 1798 – *Maj.Gen. Titov 1st's*.

Taurica Grenadiers– 31 October 1798 – *Gen.-of-Inf. Benkendorf's*; 13 September 1799 – *Maj.-Gen. Zavalishin's*; 14 September 1800 – *Maj.-Gen. Danzas's*.

Kazan Grenadiers– 31 October 1798 – *Lt.-Gen. Graf Morkov's*; 10 November 1798 – *Maj.-Gen. Tuchkov 2nd's*.

Lt.-Gen. Budkevich's Musketeers (formerly Belozersk) – 31 October 1798 – as previously, *Lt.-Gen. Budkevich's*; 30 April 1799 – *Maj.-Gen. Kulnev's*; 13 May 1799 – *Maj.-Gen. Sedmoratskii's*.

Nasheburg Musketeers– 31 October 1798 – *Maj.-Gen. Kropotov's*; 5 November 1799 – *Maj.-Gen. Vilembakhov's*; 24 December 1800 – *Maj.-Gen. Yermolov's*.

Chernigov Musketeers – 31 October 1798 – *Maj.-Gen.Essen 1st's*; 30 October 1799 - *Maj.-Gen.de Gervais's(de-Zherve)*; 2 November 1800 - *Lt.-Gen.Essen 1st's*.

Maj.-Gen. Baron Rosen's Musketeers (formerly New Ingermanland) – 31 October 1798 – as previously, *Maj.-Gen. Baron Rosen's*.

Yaroslav Musketeers – 31 October 1798 – *Maj.-Gen.Durasov's*; 11 October 1799 - *Maj.-Gen. Lasunskii 1st's*.

Apsheron Musketeers– 31 October 1798 – *Maj.-Gen. Miloradovich's*.

Smolensk Musketeers– 31 October 1798 – *Lt.-Gen.Povalo-Shveikovskii 1st's*; 10 September 1800 - *Lt.-Gen.Borozdin 1st's*; 6 October 1800 - *Maj.-Gen.Repninskii's*.

Ryazhsk Musketeers– 31 October 1798 – Maj.-Gen. Sedmoratskii's; 13 May 1799 - Lt.-Gen.Graf Langeron's (Lanzherona).

Kursk Musketeers– 31 October 1798 – *Lt.-Gen. Prshibyshevskii's*.

Baden the Elder's Musketeers(formerly Kozlov) – 31 October 1798 – as previously, *Baden the Elder's*; 20 June 1799 - *Maj.-Gen.Prince Volkonskii 2nd's*; 25 January 1800 - *Maj.-Gen.Maksheev's*.

Sevastopol Musketeers – 31 October 1798 – *Gen.-of-Inf. Graf Kakhovskii's*; 13 February 1800 - *Maj.-Gen. Serbin's*.

Belev Musketeers– 31 October 1798 – *Maj.-Gen. Mansurov 1st's*.

Aleksopol Musketeers – 31 October 1798 – *Lt.-Gen. Hagenmeister's (Gagenmeistera)*; 26 June 1800 - *Maj.-Gen.Loveika's*.

Shlüsselburg Musketeers– 31 October 1798 – *Maj.-Gen. Izmailov's*.

Bryansk Musketeers– 31 October 1798 – *Maj.-Gen. Olsufev's*; 24 September 1800 - *Maj.-Gen. Lüders' (Lidersa)*.

Troitsk Musketeers – 31 October 1798 – *Maj.-Gen. Borozdin 2nd's*.

Ladoga Musketeers – 31 October 1798 – *Lt.-Gen. Katenin's*; 5 April 1800 - *Maj.-Gen. Sukin 2nd's*.

Polotsk Musketeers – 31 October 1798 – *Maj.-Gen. Snazin's*; 7 May 1799 - *Maj.-Gen.Tinkov's*.

Archangel Musketeers – 31 October 1798 – *Maj.-Gen. Baron Delgam's*; 28 June 1799 - *Maj.-Gen. Graf Kamenskii 2nd's*.

Maj.-Gen. von Klugen's Musketeers(formerly Old Ingermanland) – 31 October 1798 – as previously, *Maj.-Gen.von Klugen's*; 2 March 1799 – *Maj.-Gen. Steingel's*; 1 August 1799 – *Maj.-Gen. Graf Razumovskii's*; 5 February 1800 – *Maj.-Gen. Engelhardt's*.

Novgorod Musketeers – 31 October 1798 – *Lt.-Gen.Graf Szembek's (Shembeka)*; 24 April 1799 – *Maj.-Gen. Fertch's*.

Nizhnii-Novgorod Musketeers– 31 October 1798 – *Lt.-Gen. Samarin 1st's*; 1 October 1799 – *Maj.-Gen. Khitrov's*.

Vitebsk Musketeers– 31 October 1798 – *Maj.-Gen. Ostrozhskii*; 16 February 1800 – *Maj.-Gen. Kassagovskii's*; 4 March 1801 – *Maj. Gen. Emme's*; 5 March 1801 – *Maj.-Gen. Musin-Pushkin's*.

Azov Musketeers – 31 October 1798 – *Maj.-Gen. Rebinder's*; 3 October 1799 – *Maj.-Gen. Selekhov's*.

Orel Musketeers– 31 October 1798 *Maj.Gen. Mansurov 2nd's*; 18 December 1799 *Maj.Gen. Brunov's*.

Reval Musketeers– 31 October 1798 – *Maj.-Gen. Khotuntsev's*.

Tula Musketeers – 31 October 1798 – *Maj.-Gen. Tyrtov's*; 9 January 1800 – *Maj.-Gen. Baron Drexel's(Drekselya)*.

Maj.-Gen. Vadkovskii's Musketeers (formerly Yelets) – 31 October 1798 – as previously, *Maj.-Gen.Vadkovskii's*; 15 October 1799 – *Maj.-Gen. de Gervais's (de-Zherve)*; 30 October 1799 – *Maj.-Gen. Vitovtov's*; 4 July 1800 – *Maj.-Gen. Yefimovich's*.

Pskov Musketeers – 31 October 1798 – Gen.-Field Marshal Prince Repnin's; 26 November 1798 – Maj.-Gen. Markov's; 27 November 1798 – Gen.-of-Inf. de Lacy's (de-Lassiya): 26 October 1799 – Gen.-of-Inf. Golenishchev-Kutuzov's.

Tambov Musketeers – 31 October 1798 – *Lt.-Gen. Ferster's (Fershtera)*.

Rostov Musketeers – 31 October 1798 – Lt.-Gen. Rimskii-Korsakov's; 24 October 1799 – Maj.-Gen. Povalo-Shveikovskii 2nd's; 26 October 1799 – Maj.-Gen. Kolokol'tsov's; Maj.-Gen. Stellikh's; 2 April 1800 – Maj.-Gen. Bussov's; 10 August 1800 – Maj.-Gen. Mitskii's.

Murom Musketeers – 31 October 1798 – *Maj.-Gen. Masalov's*; 16 November 1798 – *Maj.-Gen. Shilling 2nd's*; 17 November 1798 – *Maj.-Gen. Titov's*; 18 November 1798 – *Gen.-of-Inf. de Lacy's (de-Lassiya)*; 27 November 1798 – *Maj.-Gen. Markov 1st's*; 24 October 1799 – *Maj.-Gen. Alekseev's*; 26 October 1799 – *Maj.-Gen. Povalo-Shveikovskii 2nd's*; 23 September 1800 – *Maj.-Gen. Petrovskii's*.

Staryi-Oskol Musketeers – 31 October 1798 – *Lt.Gen. Kozlov's*; 3 January 1800 – *Maj.Gen. Bykov's*

Tobolsk Musketeers – 31 October 1798 – *Lt.-Gen. Baron Fersen's (Ferzena)*; 14 January 1801 - *Maj.-Gen.Garin's*.

Tiflis Musketeers – 31 October 1798 – *Maj.Gen. Stremoukhov's*; 8 October 1800 - *Maj.Gen.Leont'ev's*.

Voronezh Musketeers – 31 October 1798 – *Maj.-Gen. von Eckeln's (fon Ekel'na)*; 29 January 1799 - *Maj.-Gen.Arsen'ev 2nd's*.

Kazan Musketeers – 31 October 1798 – Maj.-Gen. Kiselev's; 24 February 1799 - Maj.-Gen. Briesemann von Nettig's (Brizeman-fon-Nettinga); 2 March 1799 - Lt.-Gen. Knorring 2nd's.

Moscow Musketeers – 31 October 1798 – *Lt.-Gen. Fensch's (Fensha)*.

Kabarda Musketeers– 31 October 1798 – *Maj.-Gen. Arsen'ev 1st's*; 17 December 1799 - *Maj.-Gen. Kochius's (Kokhiusa)*; 29 January 1800 - *Maj.-Gen.Gulyakov's*.

Vladimir Musketeers – 31 October 1798 – Gen.-of-Inf. Graf Gudovich 2nd's; 8 June 1800 – Gen.-of-Inf. Rosenberg's (Rozenberga).

Uglich Musketeers– 31 October 1798 – Maj.-Gen. Konovnitsyn's; 2 November 1798 – Maj.-Gen. Korf's; 20 February 1800 – Maj.-Gen. Baron Gersdorff's (Gerzdorfa).

Sevsk Musketeers– 31 October 1798 – *Maj.-Gen. Tuchkov 1st's*.

Narva Musketeers – 31 October 1798 – *Maj.-Gen. Rothof's (Rodgofa)*.

Dnieper Musketeers– 31 October 1798 – *Maj.-Gen. Arbenev's*; 24 October 1799 – *Maj.-Gen. Vyazmitinov's*; 19 May 1800 – *Maj.-Gen. Konovich's*.

Maj.-Gen. Samarin 2nd's Musketeers (formerly Vyatka) – 31 October 1798 – as previously, *Maj.-Gen. Samarin 2nd's*; 18 February 1799 – *Maj.-Gen. von Manteufel's (Manteifelya).*

Suzdal Musketeers– 31 October 1798 – *Maj.-Gen. Glazov 2nd's*; 27 May 1800 – *Maj.-Gen. Likhachev 2nd's*; 12 January 1801 – *Maj.-Gen. Shenshin's.*

Maj.-Gen. Sukov's Musketeers (formerly Kexholm) – 31 October 1798 – as previously, *Maj.-Gen. Sukov's*; 4 December 1800 - *Maj.-Gen. Verderevskii's.*

Vyborg Musketeers – 31 October 1798 – Maj.-Gen. Essen 3rd's; 18 August 1800 - Maj.-Gen. Gandza 1st's (Gandzha 1-go).

Ryazan Musketeers– 31 October 1798 – *Gen.-of-Inf. Golenishchev-Kutuzov's*; 26 October 1799 - *Maj.-Gen. Alekseev's.*

Neva Musketeers – 31 October 1798 – Lt.-Gen. Prince Volkonskii 1st's; 25 January 1800 – Lt.-Gen. Prince Gorchakov 1st's.

Velikie-Luki Musketeers– 31 October 1798 – *Maj.-Gen. Glazov 1st's*; 21 November 1799 - *Maj.-Gen. Vyatkin's*; 19 January 1800 - *Maj.-Gen. Castelli's (Kastelliya).*

Sofiya Musketeers – 31 October 1798 – *Maj.-Gen. Dokhturov's*; 22 July 1800 - *Maj.-Gen. Gavro's*; 1 January 1801 - *Maj.-Gen. Nechaev's.*

Shirvan Musketeers – 31 October 1798 - *Maj.-Gen. Prince Gorchakov's*; 1 November 1798 – *Lt.-Gen. Nefed'ev's*; 13 August 1800 – *Maj.-Gen. Prince Volkonskii 3rd's*; 15 October 1800 – *Maj.-Gen. Lavrov's.*

Perm Musketeers– 31 October 1798 – Maj.-Gen. Pushchin 2nd's; 3 January 1800 – Maj.-Gen. von Hartung's (Gartunga); 11 December 1800 – Lt.-Gen. von Ritter's.

Nizovsk Musketeers– 31 October 1798 – Maj.-Gen. L'vov 1st's; 16 January 1799 - Maj.-Gen. Baranovskii 2nd's; 28 January 1801 – Lt.-Gen. Graf Szembek's (Shembeka).

Baden the Younger's Musketeers (formerly Butyrsk) – 31 October 1798 – as previously, *Baden the Younger's*; 20 June 1799 - *Maj.-Gen. Veletskii's*; 16 September 1800 - *Maj.-Gen. Malyshkin's.*

Ufa Musketeers – 31 October 1798 – Lt.-Gen. Graf Langeron's (Lanzherona); 4 February 1799 - Maj.-Gen.Engelhardt's (Engel'gardta); 18 October 1799 - Maj.-Gen. Verderevskii's; 19 May 1800 - Maj.-Gen. Tsybul'skii's.

Rylsk Musketeers – 31 October 1798 – *Maj.-Gen. Bakhmet'ev 1st's.*

Yekaterinburg Musketeers – 31 October 1798 – *Maj.-Gen. Pevtsov's.*

Selenginsk Musketeers – 31 October 1798 – Maj.-Gen. Skobel'tsyn's; 2 November 1799 - Maj.-Gen.von Düsterloh 2nd's (Disterlo 2-go); 4 November 1799 - Maj.-Gen. Talyzin 3rd's; 27 August 1800 - Maj.-Gen. Kupferschmidt's (Kupfershmita).

Tomsk Musketeers – 31 October 1798 - Maj.-Gen. Graf Ivelich 1st's; 14 December 1798 - Maj.-Gen. Pavlutskii's; 2 November 1799 – Brigadier Lavrov's; 15 October 1800 - Maj.-Gen. Graf Tiesenhausen's (Tizengauzena); 16 October 1800 - Maj.-Gen. Prince Vyazemskii's.

Maj.-Gen. Graf Elmpt's Musketeers (formerly Arkharov's) – 31 October 1798 – as previously, *Maj.-Gen. Graf Elmpt's*; 10 March 1800 - *Maj.-Gen. Fomin's*; 11 March 1800 - *Maj.-Gen. Borozdin 1st's*; 3 May 1800 - *Maj.-Gen. Prince Gorchakov 3rd's*; 18 June 1800 *Maj.-Gen. Kupriyanov's*; 26 September 1800 - *Maj.-Gen. von Grunentals 1st's (Grinentalya 1-go)*; 27 October 1800 - *Maj.-Gen. Prince Shcherbatov's.*

Maj.-Gen. Pavlutskii's Musketeers – 31 October 1798 – as previously, *Maj.-Gen. Pavlutskii's*; 14 December 1798 – *Lt.-Gen. Graf Ivelich 1st's*; 15 December 1799 - *Maj.-Gen. Runich 1st's.*

Maj.-Gen. Brant's Musketeers – 31 October 1798 – as previously, *Maj.-Gen. Brant's*; 22 April 1799 – *Maj.-Gen. Merkulov's*; 14 December 1800 - *Maj.-Gen Kashkin's*.

Maj.-Gen. Leitner's Musketeers – 31 October 1798 – as previously, *Maj.-Gen. Leitner's*; 29 January 1800 – *Lt.-Gen. Nesvetev's*.

Maj.-Gen. Müller 1st's Musketeers – 31 October 1798 – as previously, *Maj.-Gen. Müller 1st's*.

Maj.-Gen. Marklovskii 1st's Musketeers – 31 October 1798 – as previously, *Maj.-Gen. Marklovskii 1st's*; 6 October 1800 – *Maj.-Gen. Prince Gorchakov 3rd's*; 13 October 1800 – *Maj.-Gen. Anikeev's*.

Maj.-Gen. Berg's Musketeers – 31 October 1798 – as previously, *Maj.-Gen. Berg's*; 7 February 1800 – *Maj.-Gen. Baklanovskii's*.

1st Jägers – 31 October 1798 – *Maj.-Gen. Suthoff's (Sutgofa)*.

2nd Jägers – 31 October 1798 – Maj.-Gen. Michelson 2nd's (Mikhel'sona 2-go); 10 August 1800 – Col. Steder's (Shtedera); 4 September 1800 – Maj.-Gen. Michelson 2nd's.

3rd Jägers– 31 October 1798 – *Maj.-Gen. Gvozdev's*.

4th Jägers – 31 October 1798 – *Maj.-Gen. Barclay de Tolly's*.

5th Jägers – 31 October 1798 – Maj.-Gen. Vorob'ev's; 6 March 1799 – Maj.-Gen. Titov 2nd's; 27 July 1800 – Col. Ivanov's; 18 December 1800 – Maj.-Gen. Prince Volkonskii 3rd's; 20 December – Maj.-Gen. von Bradke's.

6th Jägers– 31 October 1798 – Maj.Gen. Fock 1st's (Foka 1-go); 3 January 1800 – Maj.Gen. Alfimov's.

7th Jägers – 31 October 1798 – Maj.-Gen. Prince Bagration's; 9 June 1800 – Col. Graf Ivelich 3rd's.

8th Jägers – 31 October 1798 – *Maj.-Gen. Chubarov's*; 13 May 1799 – *Maj.-Gen. Müller's (Millera)*.

9th Jägers – 31 October 1798 – Maj.-Gen. Gramsdorf; 9 July 1800 – Col. Prioudo's (Prioudeaux?) (Priudy).

10th Jägers – 31 October 1798 – Maj.-Gen. Mainov's; 6 March 1799 – Maj.-Gen. Weidemeyer's (Veidemeiera).

11th Jägers – 31 October 1798 – *Lt.-Col. Ivanov's*; 17 January 1799 – *Maj.-Gen. Markov's*.

12th Jägers – 31 October 1798 – *Col. Balla's*; 8 May 1799 – *Maj.-Gen. Stoyanov's*; 2 March 1800 – *Maj.-Gen. Balla's*.

13th Jägers – 31 October 1798 – *Maj.-Gen. Kashkin's*; 27 September 1799 – *Maj.-Gen. Gangeblov's*.

14th Jägers – 31 October 1798 – Maj.-Gen. Baggehufvudt's (Baggovuta); 27 July 1800 – Col. Prince Vyazemskii's.

15th Jägers – 31 October 1798 – *Maj.-Gen. Kuprin's*; 27 November 1798 – *Maj.-Gen. Drashkevich's*; 15 December 1800 – *Col. Steder's (Shtedera)*.

16th Jägers – 31 October 1798 – Maj.-Gen. Nasokin's; 27 November 1798 – Maj.-Gen. Verevkin's; 4 July 1799 – Maj.-Gen. Leichner's (Leikhnera); 15 January 1800 – Maj.-Gen. Stempel's (Shtempelya).

17th Jägers – 31 October 1798 – *Maj.-Gen. Likhachev's*.

18th Jägers – 31 October 1798 – *Maj.-Gen. Lazarev's*.

19th Jägers– 31 October 1798 – Maj.-Gen. Baron Güldenskjiold's (Gil'denshol'da); 13 April 1800 – Maj.-Gen. Prince Orbelian's; 8 May 1800 – Maj.-Gen. Voeikov's.

20th Jägers – 31 October 1798 – *Maj.-Gen. Shishkov's*; 30 May 1800 – *Col. Kornitskii's*.

27 January 1800 – One more regiment was added to the field infantry, the *Senate Regiment (Senatskii polk)*, renamed from the Senate Battalion and at the same time brought to a strength of two battalions [20].

28 January 1800 – This regiment is named *Major General Martens' Musketeer Regiment*, and on 2 April 1800-renamed *Major General Ushakov's* [21].

8 March 1800 – **Suthoff's Jäger Regiment** (formerly the 1st) is disbanded [22].

27 September 1800 – Combined Grenadier battalions are ordered to be called simply *Grenadier battalions* [23]. Two Musketeer regiments were designated to be formed: *Baron Sprengtporten's (Sprengportena)* and *Sakin's*, but these never completed their organization [24].

6 October 1800 – A new Inspectorate was established: the *Kharkov Inspectorate*, which included the regiments of *Merkulov* (formed in 1798 as Maj.-Gen. Brant's), *Müller 1st* (formed 1799), and *Prince Gorchakov 3rd's* (formed 1798 as Maj.-Gen. Marklovskii 1st's [25].

(**24 January 1801** – It is confirmed that in all **Grenadier regiments** except the Leib-Grenadiers, privates in ten companies are to be called Fusiliers and in the two wing companies-Grenadiers. (HIGHEST Order of 24 January 1801). - M.C.)

In this same year yet another new Inspectorate was formed: the *Brest Inspectorate* [26].

After all these changes, at the death of EMPEROR PAUL I the regiments of field infantry were as follows:

a) Grenadiers – Leib-Grenadiers, Kerbits's (former Pavlovsk), Palitsyn's (Yekaterinoslav), Sacken 1st's (St.-Petersburg), Crown Prince of Mecklenberg's (Astrakhan), Passek's (Kiev), Prince Carl of Mecklenberg's (Moscow), Berg's (Little Russia), Bakhmetev 3rd's (Siberia), Mamaev's (Phanagoria), Titov 1st's (Kherson), Danzas's (Taurica), Tuchkov 2nd's (Caucasus).

b) Musketeers - Sedmoratskii's (Belozersk), Yermolov's (Nasheburg), Essen 1st's (Chernigov), Rosen's (New Ingermanland) Lasunskii 1st's (Yaroslav), Miloradovich's (Apsheron), Repninskii's (Smolensk), Langeron's (Ryazhsk), Prshibyshevskii's (Kursk), Maksheev's (Kozlov), Serbin's (Sevastopol), Mansurov 1st's (Belev), Loveika's (Aleksopol), Izmailov's (Shlüsselburg), Lüders'(Bryansk), Troitsk (Borozdin 2nd's), Sukin 2nd's (Ladoga), (Polotsk) Tinkov's, Graf Kamenskii 2nd's (Archangel), Engelhardt's (Old Ingermanland), Fertch's (Novgorod), Khitrov's (Nizhnii-Novgorod), Musin-Pushkin's (Vitebsk), Selekhov's (Azov), Brunov's (Orel), Khotuntsev's (Reval), Drexel's (Tula), Yefimovich's (Yelets), Golenishchev-Kutuzov's (Pskov), Ferster's (Tambov), Mitskii's (Rostov), Petrovskii's (Murom), Bykov's (Staryi-Oskol), Garin's (Tobolsk), Leont'ev's (Tiflis), Arsen'ev's (Voronezh), Knorring 2nd's (Kazan), Fensch's (Moscow), Gulyakov's (Kabarda), Rosenberg's (Vladimir), Gersdorff's (Uglich), Tuchkov 1st's (Sevsk), Rothof's (Narva), Konovich's (Dnieper), Manteufel's (Vyatka), Shenshin's (Suzdal), Verderevskii's (Kexholm), Gandza 1st's (Vyborg), Alekseev's (Ryazan), Prince Gorchakov 1st's (Neva), Castelli's (Velikie-Luki), Nechaev's (Sofiya), Lavrov's (Shirvan), Ritter's (Perm), Graf Szembek's (Nizovsk), Malyshkin's (Butyrsk), Tsybul'skii's (Ufa), Bakhmet'ev 1st's (Rylsk), Pevtsov's (Yekaterinburg), Kupferschmidt's (Selenginsk), Prince Vyazemskii's (Tomsk), Prince Shcherbatov's (formerly Arkharov's), Runich 1st's (formerly Pavlutskii's), Kashkin's (formerly Brant's), Nesvetev's (formerly Leitner's), Müller 1st's, Anikeev's (formerly Marklovskii 1st's), Baklanovskii's (formerly Berg's), Ushakov's (formerly Senate).

c) Jägers - Michelson 2nd's (formerly the 2nd), Gvozdev's (3rd), Barclay de Tolly's (4th), Bradke's (5th), Alfimov's (6th), Graf Ivelich 3rd's (7th), Müller's (8th) Prioudo's (9th), Weidemeyer's (10th), Markov's (11th), Balla's (12th), Gangeblov's (13th), Prince Vyazemskii's (14th), Steder's (15th), Stempel's (16th), Likhachev's (17th), Lazarev's (18th), Voeikov's (19th), Kornitskii's (20th).

II. CAVALRY (*Kavaleriya*)

17 November 1796 – The Heir's Cuirassier Regiment is renamed **HIS MAJESTY'S Leib-Cuirassier Regiment** (Leib-Kirasirskii EGO VELICHSTVA polk), and the Leib-Cuirassier Regiment-**HER MAJESTY'S Leib-Cuirassier Regiment**(Leib-Kirasirskii EYA VELICHESTVA polk) [27].

29 November 1796 – Prince Potemkin's Cuirassier Regiment is named, as formerly, the *Yekaterinoslav Cuirassier Regiment*, and the Military Order Horse-Grenadier Regiment-the *Little-Russia Cuirassier Regiment (Malorossiiskii Kirasirskii polk)*. The Riga, Ryazan, Yamburg, Sofiya, Glukhov, Kiev, Chernigov, Nezhin, and Starodub Carabiniers, and the Kharkov Light Horse, are renamed as *Cuirassiers*. The Narva, Kargopol, Rostov, Moscow, Ingermanland, and Seversk Carabiniers are renamed as *Dragoons*. The Mariupol, Pavlograd, Aleksandriya, Akhtyrka, Sumy, and Izyum Light Horse, and the Yelisavetgrad Horse Jäger are renamed as *Hussars*. The Tver Carabiniers, the Kinburn Dragoons, and the Kherson, Poltava, Ostrorog, and Ukraine Light Horse, as well as the Pereyaslavl, Kiev, and Taurica Horse Jäger regiments, and the Hussar squadrons with the Pskov Dragoon Regiment are all disbanded. All Hussar regiments are named after their *Chefs*. Consequently the Regular Cavalry consisted of the following 16 Cuirassier, 16 Dragoon, and 8 Hussar regiments, with an additional 2 squadrons of Hussars with the Moscow Police.

a) *Cuirassier regiments* – HIS IMPERIAL MAJESTY'S Leib-Cuirassiers, HER IMPERIAL MAJESTY'S Leib-Cuirassiers, Military Order, Yekaterinoslav, Kazan, Ryazan, Yamburg, Glukhov, Kiev, Nezhin, Sofiya, Starodub, Chernigov, Riga, Kharkhov, and Little-Russia.

b) *Dragoon regiments* – Astrakhan, Vladimir, Nizhnii-Novgorod, Pskov, St.-Petersburg, Smolensk, Taganrog, Irkutsk, Orenburg, Siberia, Ingermanland, Narva, Rostov, Moscow, Seversk, and Kargopol.

c) *Hussar regiments* – Bour's (formerly Pavlograd), Borovskii's (formerly Mariupol), Godlevskii's (formerly Aleksandriya), Shevich's (formerly Sumy), Lindener's (formerly Akhtyrka), Dunin's (formerly Yelisavetgrad), Schiets's (formerly Olviopol), and Izyum, which kept its previous name until a *chef* was appointment.

Each Cuirassier and Dragoon regiment consisted of five squadrons, while Hussar regiments consisted of ten [28].

3 December 1796 – Following the example of the Infantry, Cavalry regiments were also distributed among divisions [29]:

1. *In the St.-Petersburg Division* – both Leib-Cuirassier regiments.
2. *Moscow Division* – Yekaterinoslav and Sofiya Cuirassiers; Rostov Dragoons; Shevich's (former Sumy) and Lindener's (former Akhtyrka) Hussars.
3. *Livonia Division* – Starodub, Riga, Kazan, Kiev, and Military Order Cuirassiers, and Izyum Hussars.
4. *Smolensk Division* – St.-Petersburg and Kargopol Dragoons.
5. *Lithuania Division* – Moscow and Ingermanland Dragoons, and Godlev's (former Aleksandriya) Hussars.
6. *Finland Division* – Pskov Dragoons.
7. *Ukraine Division* – Kharkov, Little-Russia, Chernigov, Nezhin, and Yamburg Cuirassiers; Borovskii's (former Mariupol) and Bour's (former Pavlograd) Hussars.
8. *Yekaterinoslav Division* – Glukhov and Ryazan Cuirassiers; Seversk and Astrakhan Dragoons; Dunin's (former Yelisavegrad) and Schiets's (former Olviopol) Hussars.
9. *Taurica Division* – Smolensk Dragoons.

10. *Caucasus Division* – Taganrog, Nizhnii-Novgorod, Narva, and Vladimir Dragoons.

11. *Orenburg Division* – Orenburg Dragoons.

12. *Siberia Division* – Siberia and Irkutsk Dragoons.

25 December 1796 – The Izyum Hussar Regiment is named *Maj.-Gen. Zorich's Hussars*[30].

9 June 1797 – The *Tatar-Lithuanian Horse Regiment (Konnyi Tatarskii-Litovskii polk)*, consisting of ten squadrons, is formed from natives of the annexed Polish provinces [31].

26 June 1797 – The *Polish Horse Regiment (Konnyi Pol'skii polk)*, consisting of ten squadrons, is also formed from natives of those provinces [32].

15 September 1797 – Lt.-Gen. Zorich's Hussar Regiment (formerly Izyum) is named *Maj.-Gen. Annenkov's Hussar Regiment*[33].

9 October 1797 – Maj.-Gen. Godlevskii's Hussar Regiment (formerly Aleksandriya) is named *Maj.-Gen. Gizycki's (Gizhitskago) Hussar Regiment*[34].

16 October 1797 – Maj.-Gen. Borovskii's Hussar Regiment (formerly Mariupol) is named *Maj.-Gen. Prince Bagration's Hussar Regiment*[35].

13 March 1798 – Dunin's Hussar Regiment (formerly Yelisavetgrad) is named *Maj.-Gen. Voropanskii's Hussar Regiment*[36].

10 August 1798 – Maj.-Gen. Annenkov's Hussar Regiment (formerly Izyum) is named *Maj.-Gen. Tregubov's Hussar Regiment*[37].

20 August 1798 – New Cuirassier regiments are formed: Lieutenant General Neplyuev's, Major General Frederici's (Frideritsiya), and Major General Zorn's (Tsorna) New Hussar regiments are formed: Major General Schreiders 1st's and Khastatov's. Major General Czorba's (Chorby) Hussar Regiment is formed. [38].

23 September 1798 – Maj.-Gen. Prince Bagration's Hussar Regiment (formerly Mariupol) is named *Maj.-Gen. Prince Kekuatov's Hussar Regiment*[39].

30 September 1798 – The Astrakhan, Rostov, and Irkutsk Dragoon Regiments are ordered to be named after their *Chefs*: the first – *Major General L'vov's Dragoons*, the second – *Major General von Derviz's*, and the third – *Major General Sacken's* [40].

5 October 1798 – The Seversk Dragoon Regiment is named, as before, *Major General Düsterloh's (Disterlo) Dragoon Regiment*, and the Kharkov Cuirassier Regiment-*Major General Zaplatin's Cuirassier Regiment* [41].

15 October 1798 – The Riga Cuirassier Regiment is named *Major General Müller's (Millera) Cuirassier Regiment* [42].

18 October 1798 – The Yamburg Cuirassier Regiment is named *Major General Prince Chevkin's Cuirassier Regiment* [43].

25 October 1798 – Major General Zaplatin's Cuirassier Regiment (formerly Kharkov) is named *Major General Romadanovskii-Ladyzhenskii's Cuirassier Regiment*, and the Little-Russia Cuirassier Regiment-*MajorGeneral Kostylev's Cuirassier Regiment* [44].

26 October 1798 – Major General Gizycki's Hussar Regiment (formerly Aleksandriya) is named *Major General Nikorits's Hussar Regiment*[45].

31 October 1798 – All Cavalry regiments are ordered to be named after their *Chefs*. As a result they received the following titles, with subsequent changes [46]:

HIS MAJESTY'S Leib-Cuirassiers and HER MAJESTY'S Leib-Cuirassiers – kept their names.

Military Order Cuirassiers – 31 October 1798 – *Lt.-Gen. Tormasov's*; 11 July 1799 – *Maj.-Gen. Sacken 4th's*; 22 February 1800 – *Maj.-Gen. Gamper's*; 21 June 1800 – *Maj.-Gen. Prince Golitsyn 5th's*.

Yekaterinoslav Cuirassiers– 31 October 1798 – *General-Field Marshal Graf Saltykov 2nd's*.

Kazan Cuirassiers – 31 October 1798 – *Lt.-Gen. Bordakov's*; 7 February 1799 – *Maj.-Gen. Musin-Pushkin's*; 11 March 1799 – *Maj.-Gen. Leviz's*; 23 July 1800 – *Maj.-Gen. Graf Golovin's*.

Ryazan Cuirassiers – 31 October 1798 – Maj.-Gen. von Riedel's (fon-Ridelya) ; 23 October 1799 – Maj.-Gen. Chernysh's ; 17 December 1799 – Maj.-Gen. Marquis de Lambert's.

Maj.-Gen. Chevkin's Cuirssiers (formerly Yamburg) – 31 October 1798 – as previously, *Maj.-Gen. Chevkin's*; 4 June 1799 – *Maj.-Gen. Helfreich's(Gel'freikha)*; 23 January 1800 – *Maj.-Gen. Prince Gorchakov 4th's*.

Glukhov Cuirassiers– 31 October 1798 – Gen.-of-Cav. Michelson 1st's (Mikhel'sona 1-go); 13 February 1800 – Lt.-Gen. von Brincken's (Brinkena).

Kiev Cuirassiers – 31 October 1798 – *Lt.-Gen. Shuvalov's*; 21 January 1799 – *Maj.-Gen. Cozens's (Kozensa)*; 23 January 1799 – *Maj.-Gen. Svechin 3rd's*; 15 July 1800 – *Maj.-Gen. Zabolotskii's*.

Nezhin Cuirassiers– 31 October 1798 *Maj.-Gen. Gudovich 4th's*; 30 Jan. 1800 *Maj.-Gen. Berladskii's*.

Sofiya Cuirassiers– 31 October 1798 – *Lt.-Gen. Prince Golitsyn 1st's*; 27 November 1798 – *Maj.-Gen. Karab'in's*; 25 April 1799 – *Maj.-Gen. Graf Igelström's*; 9 July 1799 – *Maj.-Gen. Barkov's*.

Starodub Cuirassiers – 31 October 1798 – *Gen.of Cav. Numsen's*; 15 April 1799 – *Maj.Gen. Voinov's*.

Chernigov Cuirassiers– 31 October 1798 – *Maj.-Gen. Essen 2nd's* ; 20 December 1800 – *Lt.-Gen. Musin-Pushkin's*.

Maj.-Gen. Müller 2nd's Cuirassiers (formerly Riga) – 31 October 1798 – as previously, *Maj.-Gen. Müller 2nd's*; 7 May 1800 – *Lt.-Gen. Prince Alexander of Württemberg's*; 9 September 1800 – *Col. Khomyakov's*; 10 September 1800 – *Lt.-Gen. Prince Alexander of Württemberg's*.

Maj.-Gen. Prince Romadanovskii-Ladyzhenskii's Cuirassiers (formerly Kharkov) – 31 October 1798 – as previously, *Maj.-Gen. Prince Romadanovskii-Ladyzhenskii's*; 23 January 1799 – *Maj.-Gen. Cozens's*.

Maj.-Gen. Kostylev's Cuirassiers (formerly Little-Russia) – 31 October 1798 – as previously, *Maj.-Gen. Kostylev's*; 23 January 1799 – *Maj.-Gen. Prince Romadanovskii-Ladyzhenskii's*.

Maj.-Gen. Neplyuev 1st's Cuirassiers – 31 October 1798 – as previously, *Maj.-Gen. Neplyuev 1st's*; 8 September 1799 – *Maj.-Gen. Kamenev's*; 2 March 1800 – *Maj.-Gen. Zimmerman's (Tsimmermana)*.

Maj.-Gen. Friderici's Cuirassiers – 31 October 1798 – as previously, *Maj.-Gen. Friderici's*; 19 December 1799 – *Maj.-Gen. von Knorring 3rd's*.

Maj.-Gen. Zorn's Cuirassiers – 31 October 1798 – as previously, *Maj.-Gen. Zorn's*;

Vladimir Dragoons – 31 October 1798 – *Lt.-Gen. Obrezkov 1st's*, but from 3 April 1800 combined with the *Taganrog Regiment*.

Maj.-Gen. L'vov 2nd's Dragoons (formerly Astrakhan) 31 October 1798 as previously, *Maj.-Gen. L'vov 2nd's*.

Nizhnii-Novgorod Dragoons – 31 October 1798 – *Maj.-Gen. Grushetskii's*, but from 3 April 1800 combined with the *Narva Regiment*.

Pskov Dragoons– 31 October 1798 – Maj.-Gen. Baron von-der-Osten-Sacken 3rd's; 11 March 1799 – Prince Eugene of Württemberg's.

St.-Petersburg Dragoons– 31 October 1798 – *Maj.Gen. Shepelev's*; 27 October 1800 *Maj.Gen. Engelhardt's*.

Smolensk Dragoons – 31 October 1798 – *Maj.-Gen. von Brincken's*; 13 Feburary 1800 – *Gen.-of-Cav. Michelson 1st's*.

Taganrog Dragoons – 31 October 1798 – *Maj.-Gen. Ivashev's*; 30 November 1798 – *Maj.-Gen. Lang's*, but from 3 April 1800 combined with the *Vladimir Regiment*.

Maj.-Gen. Sacken 2nd's Dragoons (formerly Irkutsk) – 31 October 1798 – as previously, *Maj.-Gen. Sacken 2nd's*, but from 3 April 1800 combined with the *Siberia Regiment*.

Orenburg Dragoons– 31 October 1798 – *Maj.-Gen. Veovodskii's*.

Siberia Dragoons– 31 October 1798 – *Gen.-of-Cav. de Vioménil's (Deviomenilya)*; 4 February 1799 – *Maj.-Gen. Prince Odoevskii's*; 3 March 1800 – *Maj.-Gen. Zimin's*, but from 3 April 1800 combined with the *Irkutsk Regiment*.

Ingermanland Dragoons – 31 October 1798 – *Lt.-Gen. Graf Kinson's*; 14 September 1800 – *Maj.-Gen. Khomyakov's*.

Narva Dragoons – 31 October 1798 – *Lt.-Gen. Friese's (Friza)*; 26 January 1800 – *Maj.-Gen. Pushkin's*, but from 3 April 1800 combined with the *Nizhnii-Novgorod Regiment*.

Maj.-Gen. fon Derwies's Dragoons (formerly Rostov) – 31 October 1798 – as previously, *Maj.-Gen. fon Derwies's (fon-Derviza)*; 23 August 1799 – *Maj.-Gen. Schreiders 2nd's*; 13 November 1799 – *Gen.-of-Cav. Marquis d'Autichamp's (Dotishampa)*; 30 December 1799 – *vacant*; 24 January 1800 – *Maj.-Gen. Schreiders 2nd's*.

Moscow Dragoons – 31 October 1798 – *Maj.-Gen. Svechin 2nd's*; 3 May 1800 – *Maj.-Gen. Bezobrazov's*.

Maj.-Gen. fon Düsterloh's Dragoons (formerly Seversk) – 31 October 1798 – as previously, *Maj.-Gen. fon Düsterloh's*; 28 May 1800 – *Maj.-Gen. Yesipov's*.

Kargopol Dragoons – 31 October 1798 – *Lt.-Gen. Gudovich 6th's*; 18 September 1800 – *Maj.-Gen. Graf Pahlen 3rd's*.

Maj.-Gen. Schreiders 1st's Dragoons – 31 October 1798 – as previously, *Maj.-Gen. Schreiders 1st's*; 15 October 1800 – *Maj.-Gen. Glovenskii's*; 23 November 1800 – *Maj.-Gen. Müller 2nd's*.

Maj.-Gen. Khastatov's Dragoons – 31 October 1798 – as previously, *Maj.-Gen. Khastatov's*; 9 February 1799 – *Maj.-Gen. Glazenapp's*.

Lt.-Gen. Bour's Hussars (formerly Pavlograd) – 31 October 1798 – as previously, *Lt.-Gen. Bour's*.

Gen.-of-Cav. Shevich's Hussars (formerly Sumy) – 31 October 1798 – as previously, *Gen.-of-Cav. Shevich's*; 29 March 1799 – *Maj.-Gen. Lykoshin's*; 24 October 1799 – *Maj.-Gen. Golovin's*; 12 April 1800 – *Lt.-Gen. Kologrivov's*; 21 October 1800 – *Col. Glebov's*; 1 December 1800 – *Lt.-Gen. Graf Zubov's*.

Maj.-Gen. Prince Kekuatov's Hussars (formerly Mariupol) – 31 October 1798 – as previously, *Maj.-Gen. Prince Kekuatov's*; 20 June 1799 – *Maj.-Gen. Wittgenstein's*; 1 January 1801 – *Maj.-Gen. Melissino's*.

Maj.-Gen. Nikoritsa's Hussars (formerly Aleksandriya) – 31 October 1798 – as previously, *Maj.-Gen. Nikoritsa's*; 2 October 1799 – *Maj.-Gen. Telepnev's*; 5 May 1800 – *Col. Kishinskii's*.

Maj.-Gen. Tregubov's Hussars (formerly Izyum) – 31 October 1798 – as previously, *Maj.-Gen. Tregubov's*; 2 November 1798 – *Maj.-Gen. Klyucharevskii's*; 28 March 1799 – *Maj.-Gen. Bobyr's*; 14 September 1800 – *Maj.-Gen. Graf Pahlen 2nd's*.

Lt.-Gen. Lindener's Hussars (formerly Akhtyrka) – 31 October 1798 – as previously, *Lt.-Gen. Lindener's*; 18 September 1800 – *Col. Borchugov's*.

Maj.-Gen. Voropanskii's Hussars(formerly Yelisavetgrad) – 31 October 1798 – as previously, *Maj.-Gen. Voropanskii's*; 27 April 1799 – *Maj.-Gen. Sukharev's*; 10 December 1800 – *Maj.-Gen. Sacken 3rd's*.

Gen.-of-Cav. Baron Schiets's Hussars (formerly Olviopol) – 31 October 1798 – as previously, 29 March 1799 – *Gen.-of-Cav. Baron Schiets's*; 8 March 1800 – *Col. Miloradovich 2nd's*; 28 August 1800 – *Col. Chaplygin's*.

Maj.-Gen. Chorba's Hussars – 31 October 1798 – as previously, *Maj.-Gen. Chorba's*; 15 May 1799 – *Maj.-Gen. Ivanov's*; 20 January 1800 – *Maj.-Gen. Kotovitskii's*.

Lithuanian-Tatar Horse – 31 October 1798 – *Maj.-Gen. Baranovskii 1st's*; 5 November 1800 – *Maj.-Gen. Bolotnikov's*; 8 November 1800 – *Maj.-Gen. Prince Dolgorukov 4th's*; 20 January 1801 – *Maj.-Gen. Glovenskii's*.

Polish Horse – 31 October 1798 – *Lt.-Gen. Dombrowski's*; 25 June 1799 – *Maj.-Gen. Prince Ratiev's*.

2 March 1800 – of the number of **Cuirassier** regiments established in 1798, **Zimmerman's** (former Neplyuev's), **Knorring 3rd's** (former Friderici's), **Glazenapp's** (former Khastatov's), as well as **Gotovitskii's Hussars** (former Chorba's) and the previously existing **Schreiders 2nd's Dragoons** (former Rostov)-were all disbanded [47].

8 March 1800 – Still more regiments were disbanded: *Barkov's* (former Sofiya), *Berladskii's* (former Nezhin), *Prince Gorchakov 4th's* (former Yamburg), and *Marquis de Lambert's* (former Ryazan) Cuirassiers, and *L'vov 2nd's* (former Astrakhan) Dragoons [48].

31 March 1800 – The Moscow Hussar squadrons were attached to Lt.-Gen. Lindener's Hussar Regiment (former Akhtyrka) [49].

3 April 1800 – The following **Dragoon regiments** were combined so as to form ten-squadron Dragoon regiments [50]:

Obrezkov's (former Vladimir) and Lang's (former Taganrog) – as *Obrezkov's* Regiment; from 29 September 1800 – *Col. Shepelev's*, and from 22 January 1801 – *Lt.-Gen. Shepelev's*.

Pushkin's (former Narva) and Grushetskii's (former Nizhnii-Novgorod) – as *Pushkin's* Regiment, and from 15 October 1800 – *Maj.-Gen. Portnyagin's*. Sacken 2nd's (former Irkutsk) and Zimin's (former Siberia) – as *Maj.-Gen. Sacken 2nd's* Regiment, and from 11 April 1800 – *Col. Scalon's (Skalona)*.

22 January 1801 – It was directed to form the **Tsarevich of Georgia's Hussar Regiment** (Gusarskii Tsarevicha Gruzinskago polk) [51].

20 February 1801 – This regiment was named *Colonel Shepelev's Hussar Regiment* [52].

By March of 1801 the Regular Cavalry consisted of the following regiments:

a) Cuirassiers – HIS MAJESTY'S Leib-Cuirassiers, HER MAJESTY'S Leib-Cuirassiers, Prince Golitsyn 5th's (Military Order), Graf Saltykov 2nd's (Yekaterinoslav), Graf Golovin's (Kazan), Brincken's (Glukhov), Zabolotskii's (Kiev), Voinov's (Starodub), Musin-Pushkin's (Chernigov), Prince Alexander Württemberg's (Riga), Cozens's (Kharkov), Prince Romadanovskii-Ladyzhenskii's (Little-Russia), and Zorn's.

b) Dragoons, 5-squadron reg Prince Eugene of Württemberg's (Pskov), Engelhardt's (St.-Petersburg), Michelson 1st's (Smolensk), Voevodskii's (Orenburg), and Müller 2nd's (formerly Schreiders 1st's).

c) Dragoons, 10-squadron regiments – Shepelev's (from the Vladimir and Taganrog), Portnyagin's (from the Narva and Nizhnii-Novgorod), Scalon's (from the Irkutsk and Siberia).

d) Hussars – Bour's (Pavlograd), Graf Zubov's (Sumy), Melissino's (Mariupol), Kishinskii's (Aleksandriya), Graf Pahlen 2nd's (Izyum), Borchugov's (Akhtyrka), Sacken 3rd's (Yelisavetgrad), and Chaplygin's (Olviopol).

e) Horse regiments, of Poles – Glovenskii's Lithuanian-Tatar and Prince Ratiev's Polish.

III. ARTILLERY (*Artilleriya*)

27 February 1797 – The Field Artillery-consisting of: the Bombardier Regiment, 1st and 2nd Cannoneer Regiments, and the 1st and 2nd Fusilier Regiments; the 1st, 2nd, and 3rd Bombardier Battalions, and five Horse companies-was reorganized into *battalions*: *3 Siege (Osadnyi)*, *10 Field (Polevoi)*, and *1 Horse (Konnyi)*. In place of the two Pontoon companies under the artillery administration, there were established **8** *Pontoon Depots (Pontonnye Depo)*, and it was also ordered to have a *Pioneer Regiment (Pionernyi polk)* with the Artillery [53].

Each battalion consisted of five companies, and in a company it was prescribed to have guns as follows: in a Field company – 4 12-pounder unicorns (*yedinorogi*) and 4 12-pounder cannons (*pushki*), of medium and lighter proportions (*srednei i men'shei proportsii*); in a Horse company – 6 12-pounder unicorns and 6 6-pounder cannons. There was no regulation concerning the Siege Artillery [54].

Battalions were named after their *Chefs* and were as follows [55]:

Gen.-of-Art. Mellissino's Siege Battalion-from 26 December 1797 – Lt. Gen. Chelishchev's; 26 April 1799 – Maj.-Gen. Arakcheev's; 1 October 1799 – Maj.-Gen. Belichev 1st's.

Gen.-of-Art. Wulf's (Vul'fa) Siege Battalion-29 December 1797 – Lt.-Gen. Lamsdorf's; 15 October 1799 – Maj.-Gen. Rezvyi's.

Lt.-Gen. Nilus's Siege Battalion-23 November 1797 – *Maj.-Gen. Nelyubov's.*

Lt.-Gen. Bazin's Field Battalion-7 February 1798 – Maj.-Gen. Wilde's (Vil'de); 11 April 1799 – Maj.-Gen. Begichev 1st's; 1 October 1799 – Lt.-Gen. Wilde's; 27 January 1800 – Maj.-Gen. Medem's.

Lt.-Gen. Gerbel's Field Battalion-6 November 1799 – *Maj.-Gen. Bulygin's*; 13 November 1799 – *Maj.-Gen. Karab'in's.*

Lt.-Gen. Eiler's Field Battalion-4 January 1799 – Maj.-Gen. Sievers's (Siversa).

Lt.-Gen. Chelishchev's Field Battalion-21 December 1797 – Maj.-Gen. Kaptsevich's.

Maj.-Gen. Mamontov's Field Battalion-23 November 1797 – Maj.-Gen. Kuz'min's; 8 March 1799 – Maj.-Gen. Brevern's.

Lt.-Gen. Buchholz's (Bukhgol'tsa) Field Battalion-6 November 1797 – Maj.-Gen. Merkel's; 22 January 1800 – Maj.-Gen. Prince Myshetskii 1st's.

Maj.-Gen. Mordvinov's Field Battalion-18 September 1797 – Maj.-Gen. Hellwig's (Gel'vikha).

Lt.-Gen. Brigman's Field Battalion-27 December 1797 – Lt.-Gen. Ambrazantsev's; 1 October 1799 – Maj.-Gen. Karab'in's; 13 November 1799 – Maj.-Gen. Bulygins's.

Gen.-of-Art. Mertens's Field Battalion-27 December 1797 – Lt.-Gen. Baturin's.

Lt.-Gen. Brazhnikov's Field Battalion - 21 January 1797 – Maj.-Gen. Müller's; 8 March 1799 – Maj.-Gen. Brümmer's (Brimmera).

Each **Pontoon Depot** had 50 pontoons and was named according to its location: *St.-Petersburg, Riga, Smolensk, Kiev, Kherson, Azov, Kazan*, and *Moscow* [56].

The **Pioneer Regiment** consisted of two battalions, and each battalion of five Pioneer companies and one Miners and Sappers company (*rota Miner-Saperov*) [57].

12 March 1798 – It was directed that all **Grenadier and Musketeer regiments** each have one 12-pounder unicorn and four 6-pounder cannons-except for the Leib-Grenadier Regiment, which was prescribed eight 12-pounder unicorns [58].

6 March 1800 – The **Artillery with the regiments** was taken away and brought under the Artillery administration. Along with this, *Artillery regiments* were formed from the existing battalions [59]. From the battalions of Begichev 1st and Medem – *Maj.-Gen. Begichev 1st's* regiment.

- Rezvoi and Karab'in – *Maj.-Gen. Rezvyi's.*
- Sievers's and Kaptsevich's – *Lt.-Gen. Kaptsevich's.*
- Nelyubov's and Brevern's – *Maj.-Gen. Brevern's.*
- Prince Myshetskii's and Hellwig's – *Lt.-Gen. Hellwig's.*
- Bulygin's and Baturin's – *Maj.-Gen. Bulygin's.*
- Brümmer's – *Maj.-Gen. Brümmer's*, but from 3 June 1800 – *Maj.-Gen. Begichev 2nd's.*
- Bogdanov 2nd's – *Maj.-Gen. Bogdanov 2nd's.*

13 September 1800 – Regiments were ordered to be given **numbers** [60].

Begichev 1st's - 1st Artillery Regiment.
Rezvyi's   - 2nd Artillery Regiment
Kaptsevich's   - 3rd Artillery Regiment
Brevern's   - 4th Artillery Regiment
Hellwig's   - 5th Artillery Regiment
Bulygin's   - 6th Artillery Regiment
Begichev 2nd's - 7th Artillery Regiment
Bogdanov's   - 8th Artillery Regiment

Besides these regiments, of which the first seven were foot and the rest horse, during the later part of EMPEROR PAUL I's reign the Artillery also had the above-mentioned eight Pontoon Depots and the Pioneer Regiment, as well as various detachments at fortresses and Arsenals.

IV. CORPS OF ENGINEERS (*Inzhenernyi Korpus*)

24 December 1798 – In the Corps of Engineers it was ordered to have three *Siege Depots(Osadnyya Depot)*, besides which there were also the **Engineer craftsmen detachments** at fortresses. However, the **Miner Company**, **Pioneer Company**, and **Southern Borders Engineer Company** (*Inzhenernaya Yuzhnykh granits rota*) were disbanded [61].

V. GARRISONS (*Garnizon*)

20 November 1796 – From the eight Field and three Garrison battalions in Moscow there was formed the 8-battalion *Moscow Garrison*. The St.-Petersburg Garrison battalions were named the *St.-Petersburg Garrison*. Both of these were ordered to be at a field establishment strength (*na polevom polozhenii*) [62].

21 November 1796 – The *Schlüsselburg Garrison Battalion* is established [63].

27 November 1796 - With the taking of a large part of the **St.-Petersburg Garrison's** personnel to form Arkharov 1st's Musketeer Regiment, this Garrison's organization is reduced to two battalions [64].

30 November 1796 – The Moscow Garrison is ordered to be named the *Moscow Garrison Regiment* (*Moskovskii Garnizonnyi polk*) [65].

3 December 1796 – The following Garrisons are allotted to **divisions**, just as army Infantry and Cavalry forces were [66]:

In the St. Petersburg Division – St.-Petersburg Garrison.
In the Moscow Division – Moscow Garrison Regiment.

In the Livonia Division – 1st, 2nd, 3rd, and 4th Riga Battalions; Dünamünde Battalion; 1st, 2nd, 3rd, and 4th Reval Battalions.

In the Smolensk Division – 1st and 2nd Smolensk Battalions.

In the Finland Division – 1st, 2nd, 3rd, and 4th Viborg Battalions; 1st and 2nd Fredrikshamn Battalions.

In the Ukraine Division – 1st and 2nd Kiev Battalions.

In the Yekaterinoslav Division – 1st and 2nd Taganrog Battalions.

In the Orenburg Division – 1st, 2nd, 3rd, and 4th Orenburg Battalions; 1st, 2nd, and 3rd Kazan Battalions.

In the Siberia Division – 1st, 2nd, and 3rd Tobolsk Battalions; Irkutsk Battalion; 1st and 2nd Selenginsk Battalions.

The remaining Garrisons were not included in divisions.

9 January 1797 – All Garrisons were ordered to be titled regiments, named after *Chefs* [67]:

St.-Petersburg (of 2 battalions) – *Brigadier Chernyshev's* Garrison Regiment; 17 September 1797 – *Gen.-of-Inf. Vyazmitinov's*; 30 April 1799 – *Maj.-Gen. Prince Dolgorukii 2nd's*.

Moscow (of 8 battalions) – *Gen.-of-Inf. Arkharov 2nd's* Garrison Regiment; 23 April 1800 – *Maj.-Gen. Reichenberg's (Reikhenberga)*.

Viborg (of 4 battalions) – *Lt.-Gen. Wrangel's (Vrangelya)* Garrison Regiment.

Fredrikshamn (of 2 battalions) – *Maj.-Gen. Eck's (Eka)* Garrison Regiment; 8 October 1797 – *Maj.-Gen. Bem's*; 6 May 1798 – *Lt.-Gen. Bekleshov 2nd's*; 25 July 1799 – *Maj.-Gen. Baron Mal'tits's*.

Reval (of 3 battalions) – *Gen-of-Inf. Kochius's* Garrison Regiment; 5 October 1797 – *Maj.-Gen. Zakrevskii's*; 7 October 1797 – *Gen.-of-Inf. Graf de Castro-Lacerda's (de-Kastro-Latserda)*.

Riga (of 4 battalions) – *Maj.-Gen. Toll's (Tolya)* Garrison Regiment; 19 July 1797 – *Maj.-Gen. Bulgakov's*.

Archangel or **Archangelogorod** (of 2 battalions) – *Lt.-Gen. Bolotnikov's* Garrison Regiment; 2 March 1798 – *Gen.-of-Inf. Lieven's*; 6 April 1798 – *Lt.-Gen. Leccano's (Letstsano)*; 22 September 1798 – *Lt.-Gen. Prince Lobanov-Rostovskii's*; 27 December 1798 – *Maj.-Gen. Kiraev's*.

Kazan (of 3 battalions) – *Gen.-of-Inf. Prince Meshcherskii 1st's* Garrison Regiment; 25 November 1797 – *Gen.-of-Inf. de Lacy's (De-Lassiya)*; 9 September 1798 – *Maj.-Gen. Pushchin 1st's*.

Orenburg (of 4 battalions) – *Lt.-Gen. Treiden 1st's* Garrison Regiment; 12 December 1797 – *Maj.-Gen. Lebedev's*.

Tobolsk (of 3 battalions) – *Lt.-Gen. Prince Meshcherskii 2nd's* Garrison Regiment.

Smolensk (of 2 battalions) – *Lt.-Gen. Voevodskii's* Garrison Regiment; 11 September 1798 – *Maj.-Gen. Prince Dolgorukov 3rd's*; 23 December 1798 – *Maj.-Gen. Rautenstern's*.

Selenginsk (of 2 battalions) – *Col. Poltoratskii's* Garrison Regiment; 14 July 1797 – *Col. Kelch's (Kel'kha)*; 1 February 1798 – *Maj.-Gen. Blum's (Blyuma)*; 23 November 1798 – *Maj.-Gen. Buschen's*.

Kiev (of 2 battalions) – *Lt.-Gen. Wiegel's (Vigelya)* Garrison Regiment; 14 April 1798 – *Maj.-Gen. Rakhmanov 1st's*; 25 May 1798 – *Maj.-Gen. Masse's*.

Taganrog (of 2 battalions) – *Maj.-Gen. Kasporv's* Garrison Regiment; 21 August 1799 – *Col. Compati's (Kompatiya)*.

Baltic or **Rogervik** (of 1 battalion) – *Maj.-Gen. Eckbaum's* Garrison Regiment; 7 March 1799 – *Col. Theisen's (Teizena)*.

Dünamunde (of 1 battalion) – *Maj.Gen. Schilling's* Garrison Regiment; 31 December 1799 – *Col. Morokov's*.

Irkutsk (of 1 battalion, but from 16 June 1798 – of 2 battalions) – *Maj.-Gen. Blum's* Garrison Regiment; 1 February 1798 – *Gen.-of-Inf. Treiden's*; 22 September 1798 – *Lt.-Gen. Leccano's*.

Kronstadt (of 3 battalions, but from 5 January 1798 – of 4 battalions) – *Brigadier Mordvinov's* Garrison Regiment; 15 July 1797 – *Maj.-Gen. Bekleshov's*; 18 October 1798 – *Maj.-Gen. Graf Elmpt's*; 21 October 1798 – *Maj.-Gen. Ukolov's*.

Narva (of 2 battalions) – Maj.-Gen. Baron Tiesenhausen's (Tizengauzena) Garrison Regiment.

Yelisavetgrad (of 3 battalions but from 16 December 1798 – of 1 battalion) – *Maj.-Gen. Komeno's* Garrison Regiment; 8 April 1798 – *Duc de Laval-Montmorency's*; 12 April 1798 – *Maj.Gen. Dashkov's*.

St. Dimitrii Fortress (Rostov-na-Donu - M.C.) (of 3 battalions) – *Maj.-Gen. Rataev's* Garrison Regiment; 4 November 1797 – *Maj.-Gen. Vyrubov 1st's*.

Azov (of 2 battalions) – Maj.-Gen.Pecken's (Pekkena) Garrison Regiment; Maj.-Gen. Demidov's; 24 January 1799 – Maj.-Gen.Boström's (Bostrema); 31 August 1799 – Maj.-Gen. Ol'vintsev's.

Omsk (of 2 battalions) – *Lt.-Col. Chelyshkin's* Garrison Regiment; 2 November 1797 – *Maj.-Gen. Wrangel 2nd's*; 21 February 1799 – *Maj.-Gen. Balashov's*; 21 January 1800 – *Maj.-Gen. Retyunskii's*.

Astrakhan (of 4 battalions) – *Maj.-Gen.Gedeonov's* Garrison Regiment; 25 March 1798 – *Lt.-Gen. Rtishchev's*; 22 September 1798 – *Maj.-Gen. Talyzin 1st's*; 9 January 1799 – *Maj.-Gen. Prince Urusov's*; 3 March 1800 – *Maj.-Gen. Sievers's*.

Tsaritsyn (of 2 battalions) – *Lt.-Gen. Zeddelmann's (Tsedel'mana)* Garrison Regiment; 8 January 1799 – *Maj.-Gen. Cobley's (Koble)*; 8 June 1799 – *Maj.-Gen. Ievlev's*.

Kizlyar (of 2 battalions) – Maj.-Gen. Arbuzov's Garrison Regiment; 13 December 1797 – Maj.-Gen. Prince Urakov 1st's; 2 March 1799 – Maj.-Gen. Briesemann von Nettig (Brizemana-fon-Nettinga).

Schlüsselburg (of 1 battalion) – *Maj.-Gen. Kolyubakin's* Garrison Regiment; 9 September 1797 – *Maj.-Gen. Plutalov's*.

Villmanstrand (of 1 battalion) – *Maj.Gen. Stepanov's* Garrison Regiment; 4 March 1798 *Col. Rosenthal's*.

Kexholm (of 1 battalion) – Col. Hoffmann's (Gofmana) Garrison Regiment; 11 October 1797 – Col. Graf Mendoza de Butelho's (Mendozy-de-Butello); 16 December 1797 – Maj.-Gen. Smorodin's; 18 December 1797 – Col. Demidov's.

Nyslott (of 1 battalion) – *Lt.-Col. Yanysh's* Garrison Regiment.

Arensburg (of 1 battalion) – *Lt.-Col. Müller's* Garrison Regiment; 21 August 1797 – *Col. Jordan's (Iordana)*; 21 October 1798 – *Maj.-Gen. Tarbeev's*.

Pernau (of 1 battalion) – *Maj.-Gen. Kelchen's (Kel'khena)* Garrison Regiment; 25 October 1797 – *Maj.-Gen. Zubkov's*; 12 June 1799 – *Col. Baskakov's*.

Bakhmut (of 1 battalion) – *Maj.-Gen. Utkin's* Garrison Regiment; 9 April 1798 – *Col. Povalishin's*.

Tambov (of 1 battalion) – *Col. Buldakov's* Garrison Regiment; 8 April 1797 – *Col. Potrisov's*; 5 October 1797 – *Maj.-Gen. Grigor'ev 2nd's*; 6 January 1800 – *Col. Lasenkov's*.

Voronezh (of 1 battalion) – *Maj.-Gen. Sanderg's* Garrison Regiment; 29 May 1798 – *Maj.-Gen. Bibikov's*; 27 October 1799 – *Col. Nechaev's*.

Vladimir (of 1 battalion) – *Col. Schurmann's (Shurmana)* Garrison Regiment; 23 Feb.1798 – *Col. Latyshev's*.

Simbirsk (of 1 battalion) – *Maj.-Gen. Hessen's (Gessena)* Garrison Regiment.

Nizhnii-Novgorod (of 1 battalion) – *Col. Reichenberg's* Garrison Regiment.

Novgorod (of 1 battalion) – *Maj.-Gen. Nabokov's* Garrison Regiment.

Tver (of 1 battalion) – *Maj.Gen. Frenev's* Garrison Regiment; 2 March 1798 – *Col. Marklovskii 2nd's.*

Aleksandrovsk (of 1 battalion, from 17 November 1797 of 2, and from 15 February 1798 of 1 battalion) – *Maj.-Gen. Avramov's* Garrison Regiment; 9 April 1798 – *Col. Vyrubov 2nd's.*

Kirilov, later **Sudakov** (of 1 battalion) – *Col. Obernibesov's* Garrison Regiment; 13 March 1798 – *Maj. Kenkloo*; 11 May 1798 – *Col. Wimpfen's (Vimpfena).*

Petrovsk (of 1 battalion, from 17 November 1797 of 2, and from 15 February 1798 of 1 battalion) – *Lt.-Gen. Sokolov's* Garrison Regiment; 11 July 1799 – *Col. Ginkul's (Ginkulya).*

Nikitinsk, later **Balaklava** (of 1 battalion) – *Maj.-Gen. Gogolev's* Garrison Regiment.

Perekop (of 1 battalion) – *Maj.-Gen. Poyarkov's* Garrison Regiment; 8 October 1799 – *Col. Palkin's.*

Stavropol (of 1 battalion) – *Brigadier Tsyzyrev's* Garrison Regiment; 26 May 1797 – *Col. D'yakov's*; 30 December (no year – M.C.) – *Maj.-Gen. Knyshev's*; 7 March 1799 – *Col. Kondrat'ev's.*

Ozernaya, later **Orsk** (of 1 battalion) – *Maj.-Gen. Fock's (Foka)* Garrison Regiment; 9 September 1798 – *Maj.-Gen. Ucke's (Uke)*; 29 August 1799 – *Col. Winkler's (Vinklera).*

Kizilsk (of 1 battalion) – *Col. Brant 1st's* Garrison Regiment; 9 September 1797 – *Col. Shorokhov's*; 11 October 1798 – *Col. Sozonov's*; 29 October 1798 – *Col. Sendenhorst's (Sendengorsta).*

Verkhneuralsk (of 1 battalion) – *Col. Lyutov's* Garrison Regiment.

Troitsk (of 1 battalion) – *Col. Karsten's (Karshtena)* Garrison Regiment; 30 December 1797 – *Maj.-Gen. von Winkler's*; 28 September 1799 – *Col. Dreier's.*

Zverinogolovsk (of 1 battalion) – *Maj.Gen. Angelar's* Garrison Regiment; 5 July 1798 *Col. Gogel' 1st's.*

Senno, later **Pskov** (of 1 battalion) – *Brigadier Volkov's* Garrison Regiment; 10 May 1797 – *Maj.-Gen. Fürstenberg's*; 7 November 1797 – *Col. Tinkov's*; 26 November 1797 – *Maj.-Gen. Ivanov's*; 4 September 1798 – *Col. Lipinskii's*; 25 July 1799 – *Col. Tolbuzin's*; 4 August 1799 – *Col. Perskii's.*

Dünaburg (of 1 battalion) – *Col. von Grau's* Garrison Regiment; 12 July 1797 – *Maj.-Gen. Kushelev's*; 19 March 1798 – *Col. Fomin's.*

Vitebsk (of 1 battalion) – *Maj.-Gen. Graf Münnich's (Minikha)* Garrison Regiment; 9 April 1798 – *Col. Brozin's.*

Polotsk (of 1 battalion) – *Col. Duwe's (Duve)* Garrison Regiment; 7 April 1797 – *Col. Prince Khilkov's*; 20 September 1797 – *Maj.-Gen. von Bradke's*; 3 December 1798 – *Col. Ritter's.*

Mogilev, transferred to Rogachev (of 1 battalion) – *Lt.-Col. Neklyudov's* Garrison Regiment; 14 September 1798 – *Maj.-Gen. Ekesparre's*; 6 February 1799 – *Col. Bistrom's.*

Staryi-Bykhov (of 1 battalion) – *Brigadier Wenzel's (Ventselya)* Garrison Regiment; 17 September 1797 – *Maj.-Gen. Uzkov's*; 28 June 1799 – *Col. Maleev's.*

Tomsk (of 1 battalion) – *Maj.-Gen. Pelagin's* Garrison Regiment; 16 September 1797 – *Col. Yermolov's*; 29 December 1797 – *Maj.-Gen. Panov's*; 31 December 1799 – *Col. Sukhovitskii's.*

Semipalatinsk (of 1 battalion) – *Maj.-Gen. Heitzig's (Geitsiga)* Garrison Regiment; 8 September 1797 – *Col. von Grau's*; 5 July 1798 – *Col. Prince Urakov 2nd's.*

Biisk (of 1 battalion) – *Maj.-Gen. Bogdanov 3rd's* Garrison Regiment.

Petropavlovsk (of 1 battalion) – *Maj.Gen. Sverchkov's* Garrison Reg. 13 December 1798 – *Col. Putulov's.*

Mozdok (of 1 battalion) – *Maj.-Gen. Taganov's* Garrison Regiment; 22 September 1798 – *Lt.-Col. Kobrit 2nd's*; 5 September 1799 – *Col. Yunoshevskii's.*

Saratov (of 1 battalion) – *Maj.-Gen. Hartung's (Gartunga)* Garrison Regiment; 24 September 1797 – *Maj.-Gen. Kobrit 1st's.*

Of the regiments named here, the first 17, i.e. through the Irkutsk inclusive, were ordered to be maintained on a field establishment, while the rest were to be on an internal establishment. Along with this two Grenadier companies each were to be established in the regiments of Riga, Kazan, Archangel, Astrakhan, Kiev, and Kronstadt, but the Invalid companies prescribed for these unit according to the table of 1764 were abolished [68].

9 January 1797 – Fürstenberg's Garrison Regiment was transferred from Senno to Pskov [69].

25 January 1797 – In the **Riga**, **Archangel**, **Orenburg**, **Kiev**, and **Kronstadt Garrison regiments** it was directed that each have two Grenadier companies. Other Garrison regiments, except for those consisting of only one battalion, were to each have two Invalid companies [70].

23 February 1797 – The **Selenginsk Regiment** was directed to have two Grenadier companies [71].

11 April 1797 – **Fock's battalion** was transferred from the Ozernaya Fortress to **Orsk** [72].

17 November 1797 – The one-battalion **Garrison regiments** of **Gogolev** and **Obernibesov** were directed to move from the Nikitinsk to the Aleksandrovsk Fortress and from the Kirilov to the Petrovsk Fortress, respectively [73].

2 January 1798 – The battalions of the Baltic and Black-Sea Galley Fleets (*bataliony Baltiiskago i Chernomorskago Grebnykh Flotov*) were used to establish Garrison regiments: in **Rochensalm**-*Maj.-Gen. Bolotnikov's*, of three battalions; in **Sevastopol**-*Maj.-Gen. Chirkov's*, of one battalion; and in **Nikolaev**-*Maj.-Gen. Prince Vyazemskii's*, also of one battalion. All three were to be at a field establishment [74].

5 January 1798 – By newly confirmed organization tables, **Garrison battalions** were prescribed to be as follows: each field battalion-of one Grenadier and five Musketeer companies, and each internal establishment battalion-of five Musketeer and one Invalid company. Along with this the following Garrisons were transferred from an internal to a field establishment: Kronstadt, Narva, Omsk, Kizlyar, Schlüsselburg, Villmanstrand, Kexholm, Nyslott, Arensburg, Pernau, Perekop, Orsk, Kizilsk, Verkhneuralsk, Troitsk, Zverinogolovsk, Dünaburg, Tomsk, Semipalatinsk, Biisk, Petropavlovsk, and Mozdok. The Tobolsk Garrison, however, was converted to an internal establishment [75].

15 February 1798 – Gogolev's and Obernibesov's regiments, designated for transfers, are moved to **Balaklava** and **Sudak**, respectively, instead of to the Aleksandrovsk and Petrovsk fortresses [76].

16 June 1798 – To the one-battalion of Treiden's Regiment (in **Irkutsk**) is added another battalion [77].

3 October 1798 – One battalion from *Leccano's Garrison Regiment*, in **Irkutsk**, is transferred to **Nizhne-Kamchatsk** and named *Colonel Somov's Garrison Regiment*. To replace it, a new battalion is formed in Irkutsk [78].

16 December 1798 – Of the three **Yelisavetgrad** battalions, two are transferred to **Kherson** where they form *Dashkov's* Garrison Regiment [79].

3 September 1799 – The one battalion of Gogolev's Garrison Regiment (in **Balaklava**) was designated for the fortress on **Corfu** [80].

4 March 1800 – The following were disbanded: the single-battalion Garrison regiments in Baltic Port, Yelisavetgrad, Bakhmut, the Aleksandrovsk and Petrovsk fortresses, Sudak, Stavropol, Dünaburg, Polotsk, Staryi-Bykhov, and Mozdok; the two-battalion regiment in Kizlar; one battalion each from the garrisons in Kazan, Tobolsk, Smolensk, Dimitrievsk, and Azov; two battalions each from the garrisons in Viborg, Orenburg, and Astrakhan; and the St.-Petersburg Regiment [81]. From the

remaining garrisons, except in Moscow, Riga, Kronstadt, and Nizhne-Kamchatsk, and Gogolev's Regiment in Corfu, the following regiments were formed [82]:

From the regiments of Lt.-Gen. Baron Tiesenhausen (in **Narva**), Maj.-Gen. Nabokov (in **Novgorod**), Col. Perskii (in **Pskov**), and Maj.-Gen. Marklovskii 2nd (in **Tver**) - *Maj.-Gen. Marklovskii 2nd's* Regiment; from 30 October 1800 – *Colonel Frolov's*; from 1 November 1800 – *Maj.-Gen. Marklovskii 2nd's*; from 13 December 1800 – *Lt.-Gen. Vyrubov 1st's*.

From the regiments of Maj.-Gen. Plutalov (in **Schlüsselburg**), Col. Rosenthal (in **Villmanstrand**), Col. Demidov (in **Kexholm**), and Lt.-Col. Yanysh (in **Nyslott**) – *Maj.-Gen. Plutalov's* Regiment.

From the regiments of Maj.-Gen. Wrangel (in **Viborg**) and Maj.-Gen. Mal'tits (in **Fredrikshamn**) – *Gen.-of-Inf. Wrangel's* Regiment; 8 March 1800 – *Lt.-Gen. Prince Gorchakov 1st's*; 18 August 1800 – *Lt.-Gen. Essen 3rd's*.

From the regiments of Bolotnikov (in **Rochensalm**) and Tarbeev (in **Arensburg**) – *Maj.-Gen. Bolotnikov's* Regiment.

From the regiments of Graf de Castro-Lacerda's (in **Reval**) and Baskakov (in **Pernau**) – *Gen.-of-Inf. Graf de Castro-Lacerda's* Regiment; 22 May 1800 – *Lt.-Gen. Rebinder's*; 18 June 1800 – *Maj.-Gen. Prince Gorchakov 3rd's*; 6 October 1800 – *Maj.-Gen. Marklovskii 1st's*; 27 November 1800 – *Maj.-Gen. Balashov's* [83].

From the regiments of Morokov (in **Dünamünde**), Rautenstern (in **Smolensk**), Brozin (in **Vitebsk**), and Bistrom (in **Mogilev**) – *Lt.-Gen. Prince Ghica's (Gika)* Regiment.

From the regiments of Masse (in **Kiev**) and Dashkov (in **Kherson**) – *Maj.-Gen. Masse's* Regiment.

From the regiments of Prince Vyazemskii (in **Nikolaev**), Palkin (in **Perekop**), and Chirkov (in **Sevastopol**) – *Maj.-Gen. Prince Vyazemskii's* Regiment; 15 September 1800 – *Col. Koshlev's*.

From the regiment of Kompatii (in **Taganrog**), Vyrubov 2nd (in the **fortress of St. Dimitrii**), and Ol'vintsev (in **Azov**) – *Maj.-Gen. Ol'vintsev's* Regiment.

From the regiments of Sievers (in **Astrakhan**), Ievlev (in **Tsaritsyn**), and Hessen (in **Simbirsk**) – *Gen.-of-Inf. L'vov's* Regiment; 17 October 1800 – *Maj.-Gen. Graf Lieven 3rd's*.

From the regiments of Lebedev (in **Orenburg**), Lasenkov (in **Tambov**), and Nechaev (in **Voronezh**) – *Lt.-Gen. Lebedev's* Regiment.

From the regiments of Kobrit 1st (in **Saratov**), Winkler 2nd (in the **Orsk fortress**), Gogel' 1st (in **Zverinogolovsk**), and Sendenhorst (in the **Kizilsk fortress**) – *Maj.-Gen. Gogel' 1st's* Regiment; 30 November 1800 – *Maj.-Gen. Korf 1st's*.

From the regiments of Prince Urakov 2nd (in Semipalatinsk), Putilov (in the **St.-Peter Fortress**), Lyutov (in **Verkhne-Uralsk**), and Dreier (in the **Troitsk fortress**) – *Maj.-Gen. Lyutov's* Regiment; 23 June 1800 – *Col. Hesse's (Gesse)*; 9 July 1800 – *Col. Sendenhorst's*; 8 November 1800 – *Maj.-Gen. Tsyzyrev's*.

From the reg.of Retyunskii (in **Omsk**), Bogdanov 3rd's (in **Biisk**), and Sukhovitskii (in **Tomsk**) –*Maj. Gen. Retyunskii's* Reg. Along with this one of the Omsk battalions was transferred to the Zhelezinsk fortress [84].

From the regiments of Leccano (in **Irkutsk**) and Bushen (in **Selenginsk**) – *Gen.-of-Inf. Leccano's* Regiment.

From the regiments of Pushchin 1st (in **Kazan**) and Prince Meshcherskii 2nd (in **Tobolsk**) – *Lt.-Gen. Pushchin 1st's* Regiment.

From the regiments of Kiraev (in **Archangel**), Latyshev (in **Vladimir**), and Reichenberg (in **Nizhnii-Novgorod**) – *Lt.-Gen. Graf Lieven 1st's* Regiment.

Simultaneously with this reorganization, all **Garrison Grenadier companies** were disbanded except for those in the Archangel, Kronstadt, Omsk, Tomsk, Nizhne-Kamchatsk regiments, and Gogolev's regiment (in Corfu) [85].

There were no further changes in the number or composition of Garrisons during the reign of EMPEROR PAUL I.

VI. GUARDS INFANTRY (*Gvardeiskoi pekhota*)

9 November 1796 – The foot battalions that were part of the **Gatchina force** were merged into the Life Guards: of His Highness the Heir's and Arakcheev's battalions – into the Preobrazhenskii; Grand Duke ALEXANDER PAVLOVICH'S and Nedobrov's battalions – into the Semenovskii; Grand Duke CONSTANTINE PAVLOVICH'S and Malyutin's – into the Izmailovskii. The Jäger company of the Gatchina force and the Jäger detachments of the Semenovskii and Izmailovskii regiments went to form the three-company *Life-Guards Jäger Battalion (Leib-Gvardii Yegerskii batalion)* [86]. Along with this the current composition of Guards foot regiments was changed, and they were ordered to be: Preobrazhenskii-of three five-company Musketeer battalions and one three-company Grenadier battalion, while the Semenovskii and Izmailovskii were each to be of two five-company Musketeer battalions and two Grenadier companies [87].

24 January 1797 – After the example of Army infantry, *Combined* **Guards Grenadier battalions** were organized-one from the Grenadier battalion of the Life-Guards Preobrazhenskii Regiment, and another from the Grenadier companies of the Semenovskii and Izmailovskii Regiments [88].

15 April 1797 – To each of the **Guards infantry regiments** are added another five-company Musketeer battalion and one Grenadier company. The latter joined the Combined battalions which then consisted of: in the Preobrazhenskii Regiment-of four companies; in the Semenovskii and Izmailovskii Regiments-each of three companies [89].

16 September 1797 – The Combined Grenadier Battalion of the **Life-Guards Preobrazhenskii Regiment** was reinforced with a fifth company [90].

3 December 1797 – The Grenadier companies of the **Life-Guards Semeovskii** and **Izmailovskii Regiments** that had formed a Combined battalion for each of them were disbanded, and the first Musketeer, or *Chef's*, battalions, otherwise known as the *Leib-Battalions*, of the these regiments were changed to Grenadiers. Each regiment then consisted of one Grenadier and two Musketeer battalions [91].

4 December 1797 – The Leib-Battalion of the **Life-Guards Preobrazhenskii Regiment** was changed to Grenadiers [92].

10 July 1798 – The Combined Grenadier Battalion of the **Life-Guards Preobrazhenskii Regiment** was taken back into the regiment, which then in its entirety consisted of two Grenadier and three Musketeer battalions [93].

29 June 1799 – For lower ranks in the Life-Guards who are unfit for field service, the *Life-Guards Garrison Battalion(Leib-Gvardii Garnizonnyi batalion)* established, of three companies [94].

In March 1800 – Life-Guards regiments began to be named after their Chefs: Preobrazhenskii-HIS

IMPERIAL MAJESTY'S Life-Guards Regiment; Semenovskii-His Imperial Highness Alexander Pavlovich's Life-Guards Regiment; Izmailovskii-His Imperial Highness Constantine Pavlovich's Life-Guards Regiment. At the same time, Musketeer battalions of these regiments were changed to Grenadiers [95].

30 March 1800 – A fourth company was formed in the **Life-Guards Jäger Battalion** [96].

28 May 1800 – His Imperial Highness Constantin Pavlovich's Life-Guards Regiment was to be called *His Imperial Highness Nicholas Pavlovich's Life-Guards Regiment*[97].

In 1800 – **HIS IMPERIAL MAJESTY'S Life-Guards Regiment** was reduced by one battalion. At the same time, **Grenadier companies** were established for this regiment as well as the other two regiments of Guards infantry. These companies were not part of the battalions and were titled *wing, or flank, companies (fligel-roty)*, two for HIS MAJESTY'S Regiment and one each for the regiments of Their Highnesses [98].

After all these changes, by 1801 the Guards infantry consisted of:

1) *HIS IMPERIAL MAJESTY'S Life-Guards Regiment* - of four Grenadier battalions of five companies each, and two flank companies.

2) *His Imperial Highness Alexander Pavlovich's Life-Guards Regiment* – of three Grenadier battalions of five companies each, and one flank company.

3) *His Imperial Highness Nicholas Pavlovich's Life-Guards Regiment* – of three Grenadier battalions of five companies each, and one flank company.

4) Life-Guards Jäger Battalion – of four companies.

5) Life-Guards Garrison Battalion – of three companies.

VII. GUARDS CAVALRY (Gvardeiskaya kavaleriya)

7 November 1796 – From the Leib-Hussar Squadron and Cossack Convoy Command at the HIGHEST Court, and from the Hussar and Cossack regiments of the Gatchina force, there was formed a four-squadron regiment called the *Leib-Cossack Regiment*[99].

9 November 1796 – The Cuirassier, or Gendarme, and Dragoon regiments of the **Gatchina force** were put into the Life-Guards Horse Regiment [100].

11 November 1796 – Independently of the Cavalier Guards Corps in existence since 1762, a new *Cavalier Guards Corps (Kavalergardskii Korpus)* was established, consisting of one squadron [101].

14 November 1796 – The **Leib-Hussar Cossack Regiment** was ordered to be considered on the same basis with (*schitat' na odnom osnovanii s*) the Life-Guards Horse Regiment [102].

13 December 1796 – The Hussars in the Leib-Hussar Cossack Regiment were ordered to be named the *Leib-Hussar Regiment (Leib-Gusarskii polk)* and, as before, consist of two squadrons. Until further direction, the Cossacks were to remain with the regiment, under the name of the *Leib-Cossack Squadron(Leib-Kazachii eskadron)* [103].

31 December 1796 – In place of the Cavalier Guards Corps that was being formed, it was ordered to have two *Cavalier Guards squadrons (Kavalergardskie eskadrony)* [104].

28 January 1797 – The **Cavalier Guards** were ordered to have three squadrons [105].

15 April 1797 – The **Life-Guards Horse Regiment** was ordered to consist of two five-squadron battalions, and to the Leib-Hussars was added another, third, squadron [106].

30 October 1797 – The Cavalier Guard squadrons were disbanded [107].

24 January 1798 – From the two Leib-Cossack squadrons with the Leib-Hussar Regiment there was formed a *Leib-Cossack Regiment (Leib-Kazachii polk)* in its own right [108].

9 September 1798 – The **Leib-Hussar Regiment** was reformed into two battalions, each of five squadrons [109].

11 January 1799 – Upon EMPEROR PAUL I's assumption of the rank of Grand Master of the Sovereign Order of St. John of Jerusalem, a single-squadron *Cavalier Guards Corps (Kavalergardskii Korpus)* was established as a guard to the person of the Grand Master [110].

18 March 1799 – Three more squadrons was added to the **Leib-Cossack Regiment** [111].

24 May 1799 – The **Leib-Cossack Regiment** was ordered to consist of three squadrons instead of five [112].

2 February 1800 – The **Life-Guards Horse Regiment** was ordered to consist of five squadrons instead of ten [113].

15 March 1800 – The Cavalier Guards Corps was reformed into the three-squadron *Cavalier Guards Regiment (Kavalergardskii polk)*, and from this time began to be considered the equal of the Life-Guards Horse Regiment [114].

In March 1800 – The Life-Guards Horse Regiment was named **His Imperial Highness Nicholas Pavlovich's Life-Guards Regiment** (Leib-Gvardii Ego Imperatorskago Vysochestva Nikolaya Pavlovicha polk) [115].

28 May 1800 – HIS IMPERIAL HIGHNESS NICHOLAS PAVLOVICH'S Life-Guards Regiment was named *HisImperial Highness Constantine Pavlovich's Life-Guards Regiment* [116].

9 September 1800 - HIS IMPERIAL HIGHNESS CONSTANTINE PAVLOVICH'S Life-Guards Regiment, upon the naming of General of Cavalry Prince Alexander of Württemberg as *Chef*, took its previous title of the *Life-Guards Horse Regiment* [117].

10 September 1800 – With the TSESAREVICH AND GRAND DUKE CONSTANTINE PAVLOVICH being named *Chef* of the Life-Guards Horse Regiment for the second time, it again began to be called *HisImperial Highness Constantine Pavlovich's Life-Guards Regiment* [118].

After all these changes that occurred in the composition and titles of the forces in the Guards Cavalry, by 1801 it consisted of:
1) Cavalier Guards Regiment-of three squadrons.
2) His Imperial Highness Constantine Pavlovich's Life-Guards Regiment-of five squadrons.
3) *Leib-Hussar Regiment*-of two five-squadron battalions.
f) *Leib-Cossack Regiment*-of three squadrons.

VIII. GUARDS ARTILLERY (*GvardeiskayaArtilleriya*)

9 November 1796 – From the Bombardier Company of the Life-Guards Preobrazhenskii Regiment, the gunners (*pushkari*) or artillerymen (*artilleristy*) of all three regiments of Guards infantry, and the Artillery Company of the Gatchina force, there was formed the *Life-Guards Artillery Battalion (Leib-Gvardii Artilleriiskii batalion)*, divided into three foot companies and one horse company [119].

10 July 1798 – To the four companies that make up the Life-Guards Artillery Battalion are added three commands (*komandy*): **Pioneer**, **Pontoon**, and **Supply Train** (*Pionerskaya, Pontonskaya i Furshtatskaya*) [120].

15 April 1799 – The **Life-Guards Artillery Battalion** was brought to an establishment of five foot companies and one horse company [121].

30 January 1801 – The Life-Guards Artillery Battalion was ordered to be named simply **His Imperial Highness Michael Pavlovich's Artillery Battalion**(Artilleriiskii Ego Imperatorskago Vysochestva Mikhaila Pavlovicha batalion) [122].

IX. MILITARY EDUCATIONAL ESTABLISHMENTS (*Voenno-Uchebnyya zavedeniya*)

8 December 1796 – The **Corps of Foreign Co-Believers**, or **Greek Corps** (*Korpus Chuzhestrannykh Yedinovertsev, ili Grecheskii*), was disbanded [123].

16 January 1797 – The **Army Cadet Corps** (*Sukhoputnyi Kadetskii Korpus*), instead of being divided into five age groups (*vozrasty*), was organized into the same number of companies-a Grenadier and four Musketeer-and a Boys' Section (*Maloletnee otdelenie*) [124].

25 September 1797 – For the education of the children of lower military ranks serving in Garrison regiments and Provincial government companies and commands, as well as of retired lower ranks, there were established at the Garrisons some 63 *Garrison schools* (*Garnizonnyya shkoly*); in St. Petersburg-for 500 pupils; in Moscow-for 1000; in Narva, Novgorod, Archangel, Nizhnii-Novgorod, Tver, Simbirsk, Vladimir, Voronezh, Tambov, Smolensk. Polotsk, Senno, Kiev, Tsaritsyn, Kazan, Verkhneuralsk, Saratov, Stavropol, Tobolsk, Omsk, Petropavlovsk, Irkutsk, and Selenginsk-for 100 pupils for each battalion; in Kronstadt, Schlüsselburg, Riga, Reval, Dünamünd, Baltic Port, Pernau, Orenburg, Dünaburg, Vitebsk, Starobykhov, Rogachev, Viborg, Fredrikshamn; Villmanstrand; Kexholm, Nyslott, Yelisavetgrad, Taganrog, and Bakhmut, in the Aleksandrovsk, Nikitinsk, Kirilov, and Petrovsk fortresses, in Perekop, Astrakhan, the Rostov fortress of St. Dmitrii, Azov, Kizlyar, Mozdok, Orenburg, Orsk, Kizilsk, Troitsk, Zverinogolovsk, Biisk, Tomsk, and Semipalatinsk-for 50 pupils for each battalion [125].

In 1797 – The Shklov Nobles School (*Shklovskoe Blagorodnoe Uchilishche*), founded in 1778 by General Zorich on his own initiative, acquired government sponsorship and was named the *Shklov Cadet Corps* (*Shklovskii Kadetskii Korpus*) [126].

28 December 1798 – In St. Petersburg, for upbringing the children of poor nobles, field and company-grade officers, and lower ranks of the Guards, Army, and Artillery, primarily orphans, there was established the *IMPERIAL Military Orphans' Home* (*IMPERATORSKII Voenno-Sirotskii Dom*), of two sections: Nobles' and Soldiers' (*Dvoryanskoe i Soldatskoe*). Garrison schools were titled *Sections of the IMPERIAL Military Orphans' Home* (*Otdeleniya IMPERATORSKAGO Voenno-Sirotskago Doma*) [127].

10 March 1800 – The Army Cadet Corps was ordered to be called the *1st Cadet Corps* (*1-i Kadetskii Korpus*), and the Artillery and Engineers Cadet Corps-the *2nd Cadet Corps*(*2-i Kadetskii Korpus*) [128].

10 October 1800 – The Shklov Cadet Corps was named a section of the *Grodno Cadet Corps* (*Grodnenskii Kadetskii Korpus*) (proposed to be established) [129].

X. COSSACK TROOPS (*Kazach'ya voiska*)

22 November 1796 – The 3rd Chuguev Cossack Regiment is disbanded [130].

3 April 1797 – It was ordered that a ten-squadron regiment, called the *Pinsk Regiment*, be formed from Tatars who for generations had been settled in the Lithuanian provinces annexed by Russia.

The formation was to be on the same basis as the Chuguev regiments, but this whole project was not realized [131].

9 January 1798 – The **1st** and **2nd Chuguev Regiments** were ordered to each consist of ten squadrons [132].

12 July 1798 – The **Ufa Regiment**, formed in 1791 from Teptyars and landless peasants (*bobyli*) of Ufa Province, was divided into two regiments: the *1st* and *2nd Teptyar* [133].

4 September 1798 – The **Ural Cossack Sotnia** was directed to be directly attached to the IMPERIAL Person and named the *Leib-Ural Sotnia (Leib-Ural'skaya sotnya)* [134].

31 October 1798- Following the example of Army Cavalry regiments, both Chuguev regiments were ordered to be named after their *Chefs*: the 1st-*Major General Leslie's Chuguev Cossack Regiment(Chuguevskii Kazachii General-Maiora Lesliya polk)*, but from 11 November of the same year *Lieutenant-General Gorich's*; the 2nd-*Major General Neklyudov's Chuguev Cossack Regiment(Chuguevskii Kazachii General-Maiora Neklyudova polk)*, but from 3 December 1799, *Major General Sinitsyn's*[135].

6 March 1800 – From the two Chuguev Cossack regiments it was ordered to form one ten-squadron regiment with the name *Major General Sinitsyn's Chuguev Cossack Regiment* [136].

Besides these changes, during EMPEROR PAUL I'S reign the **Yekaterinoslav Cossacks** were abolished.

XI. NATIONAL TROOPS (*Natsional'nyya voiska*)

16 December 1796 – The **Taurica National divisions** (*Tavricheskie Natsional'nye diviziony*) were disbanded [137]. (*divzion* = double squadron – M.C.)

30 December 1796 – The Greek Regiment was ordered to be named the *Greek Battalion(Grecheskii batalion)*, and another Infantry battalion on the same basis as the Greek unit was to be formed from Albanians (*Albantsy*), if such were to be found settled in the New Russia territory [138].

13 April 1797 – The **Greek Battalion**, also known as the Greek Infantry Battalion, is brought to a strength of three companies [139].

20 May 1797 – The **Greek Division** (*Grecheskii division*) established in 1795 is disbanded [140].

29 October 1797 – For its permanent settlement, the Greek Battalion was given land around the town of Balaklava, and from this time on it began to be called the *Balaklava Greek Infantry Battalion (Balakavskii Grecheskii Pekhotnyi batalion)* [141].

27 November 1797 – The **Prince Condé's corps** was taken into Russian service, consisting of the following five regiments:
1) Prince Condé's French Noble Regiment (Frantsuzskii Dvoryanskii Printsa Konde polk / Régiment noble à pied de Condé).
2) Duke de Bourbon's French Grenadier Regiment (Frantsuzskii Grenaderskii Gertsoga Burbons polk / Régiment des grenadiers de Bourbon).
3) Duke of Hohenlohe's German Regiment (Nemetskii Gertsoga Gogenlo polk / Régiment d'Hohenlohe).
4) Duke de Berry's Noble Dragoon Regiment (Dvoryanskii Dragunskii Gertsoga de-Berri polk / Régiment noble à cheval d'Berry).

5) Duke d'Enghien's Dragoon Regiment (Dragunskii Gertsoga d'Angien polk / Régiment des dragons d'Enghien)[142].

The Prince Condé's Regiment consisted of two five-company Musketeer battalions; the Duke of Bourbon's Regiment-of two five-company Grenadier battalions; Hohenlohe's Regiment-of two five-company Musketeer battalions and two Grenadier companies. The remaining two regiments were of five squadrons each [143].

23 February 1800 – The **Prince Condé's corps** was disbanded [144], and during the rest of EMPEROR PAUL I's reign the only national troops were: the *Balaklava Battalion* and the *Mozdok Mountain Command (Gorskaya Mozdokskaya komanda)*, established in 1765. The **Belorussian**, **Mogilev**, and **Polotsk Standards** that existed under EMPRESS CATHERINE II were disbanded at the beginning of EMPEROR PAUL I's reign, but what day, month, and year are unknown.

XII. TEMPORARY FORCES (*Vremennyya voiska*)

18 November 1796 – The **Corps of Little-Russian Foot Marksmen** (*Korpus Malorossiiskikh peshikh strelkov*), mustered in 1794, was disbanded [145].

19 December 1797 – The **Cossack regiment of wagon drivers** (*Kazachii polk iz yamshchikov*), established in 1788, was likewise disbanded [146].

Subsequently there were no similar troops formed under special military circumstances.

XIII. SPECIAL DETACHMENTS AT VARIOUS OFFICIAL PLACES AND GOVERNMENT BUILDINGS, AND OTHER SEPARATE UNITS UNDER ARMY ADMINISTRATION.

(*Osobyya komandy, pri raznykh prisutstvennykh mestakh i kazennykh domakh i drugiya otdel'nyya chasti voennago vedomstva*)

13 December 1796 – **Feldjägers** (Fel'd"yegerya) and a **detachment of attendants for the Army hospital** (komanda sluzhitelei pri Sukhoputnom gospitale) were established [147]. (Feldjägers = military couriers. M.C.)

22 December 1796 – The *Mines Collegium Foot Company* (*Pekhotnaya rota pri Berg-Kollegii*), disbanded in 1783, was re-established [148].

16 February 1797 – The two-company **Senate Battalion** was ordered to consist of four companies [149].

5 June 1797 – The **Garrison company at the construction of the Moscow Kremlin Palace** (Garnizonnaya rota pri stroenii Moskovskago Kremlevskago Dvortsa) established in 1773, was disbanded [150].

20 July 1797 – The **Ladoga Canal battalion** was titled the *Labor Command* at this canal (*Rabochaya, pri Ladozhskom kanale, komanda*) [151].

12 August 1797 – One more company was added to the **Senate Battalion's** four existing ones [152].

2 November 1797 – An *Invalid command (Invalidnaya komanda)* was established at the **Senate's Survey Department** (*Mezhevoi Senata Departament*) [153].

5 January 1798 – The Infantry companies of the **Commissariat and Provisioning Departments** were disbanded, and in their place it was directed to have a *service personnel detachment (komanda sluzhitelei)* in each of the departments [154].

21 April 1798 – One *Invalid command* apiece was established at the **Olonets**, **Kronstadt**, and **Lugansk foundry works** (*liteinye zavody*) [155].

17 March 1799 – The **Senate Battalion** was reorganized into one Grenadier and five Musketeer companies [156].

16 April 1799 – *Invalid commands* were established as follows: one at the **Postal Department** (*Pochtovyi Departament*) and one each at the **St.-Petersburg**, **Moscow**, **Little-Russia**, **Lithuania**, **Tambov**, and **Kazan post offices** (*pochtamty*) [157].

12 November 1799 – An *Invalid command* made up of men on foot and horse was established for the **St.-Petersburg granaries** [158].

27 January 1800 – The **Senate Battalion** was reformed into a two-battalion regiment which then became part of the Army infantry [159].

XIV. STATE COMPANIES AND COMMANDS. (*Shtatnyya roty i komandy*)

31 December 1796 – Provincial organizational tables, confirmed by HIGHEST AUTHORITY, prescribed that **State provincial** *companies* and likewise **State provincial** *commands* be kept on their previous basis in the following places: in St.-Petersburg Province – 7, Moscow – 11, Novgorod – 12, Tver – 9, Pskov – 6, Smolensk – 9, Tula – 9, Kaluga – 9, Yaroslavl – 9, Kostroma – 11, Vladimir – 10, Nizhnii-Novgorod 10, Vologda – 10, Archangel – 8, Vyatka – 10, Kazan – 10, Perm – 10, Orenburg – 12, Simbirsk – 10, Penza – 10, Astrakhan – 10, Voronezh -10, Saratov 10, Tambov 10, Ryazan 10, Kursk – 9, Orel – 10, Slobodsko-Ukraine – 10, New-Russia – 10, Little-Russia – 12, Minsk – 12, Belorussia – 16, Volhynia 12, Podolia – 12, and Kiev 12 [160]. Subsequently more such companies and commands were established in the following provinces:

6 February 1797 – Lithuania – 19 [161].

19 February 1797 – Courland – 8 [162].

26 February 1797 – Viborg – 6, Estonia – 4, and Livonia – 5 [163].

4 March 1797 – Tobolsk – 16, and Irkutsk – 17 [164].

There were no changes in these numbers during the rest of EMPEROR PAUL I's reign, so they totaled 41 companies in provincial capitals and 380 commands in district seats (*uezdnye goroda*) [165].

XV. NON-SERVING INVALIDS. (*Ne sluzhashchie Invalidy*)

There were **no changes** in the number or organization of non-serving Invalid commands during EMPEROR PAUL I's reign [166].

XVI. NAVAL TROOPS. (*Morskiya voiska*)

13 November 1796 – The **Marine reg.** (*Morskie polki*) of the Baltic Fleet, the **Black-Sea Grenadier Corps**, and the **Bombardier battalions** of both fleets were put under Naval administration, as previously [167].

NOTES

(1) Directive of the War Collegium, 7 November 1796.

(2) Historical journal of the Pavlov Grenadier Regiment, sent from this regiment to the War Collegium in 1799.

(3) Highest Order.

(4) Complete Collection of Laws of the Russian Empire (Polnoe Sobranie Zakonov Rossiiskoi Imperii, hereafter PSZ), Vol. XXVI, №15,777, pg. 13.

(5) PSZ, Vol. XLIII, Part I, Section 1, Reign of EMPEROR PAUL I, pg. 1, and HIGHEST confirmed personnel authorization tables (shtaty) for Army regiments and garrisons, 29 November 1796.

(6) PSZ, Vol. XLIII, Part I, Sect. 1, pg. 2.

(7) Ibid., pgs. 6 and 7.

(8) Ibid., pg. 9.

(9) HIGHEST Orders and Chronicle of the Russian Imperial Army (Khronika Rossiiskoi IMPERATORSKOI Armii), compiled by HIGHEST direction by Prince Dolgorukii, St.-Petersburg, 1799.

(10) Ditto.

(11) Ditto.

(12) Ditto.

(13) Ditto.

(14) Ditto.

(15) Ditto.

(16) Ditto.

(17) Ditto.

(18) Ditto.

(19) Ditto.

(20) Ditto.

(21) Ditto.

(22) Signed order to the War Collegium.

(23) Highest Orders.

(24) Ditto.

(25) Ditto.

(26) No information was found regarding the month and day this Inspectorate was established.

(27) Highest Order.

(28) PSZ, Vol. XXIV, №. 17,597, pg. 27 et seq.; Vol. XLIII, Part I, Section One, pg. 1, and Highest confirmed authorization tables for Army regiments and garrisons, 29 November 1796.

(29) PSZ, Vol. XLIII, Part I, Sect. One, pg. 1.

(30) Submittal by General Field-Marshal Graf Saltykov to the War Collegium, 20 December 1796.

(31) HIGHEST Orders and Chronicle of the Russian Imperial Army, compiled by Prince Dolgorukii.

(32) Ditto.

(33) Ditto.

(34) Ditto.

(35) Ditto.

(36) Ditto.

(37) Ditto.

(38) Ditto.

(39) Ditto.

(40) Ditto.

(41) Ditto.

(42) Ditto.

(43) Ditto.

(44) Ditto.

(45) Ditto.

(46) Ditto.

(47) Signed orders to the War Collegium.

(48) Ditto.

(49) HIGHEST Orders and Chronicle of the Russian Imperial Army, compiled by Prince Dolgorukii.

(50) Ditto.

(51) Ditto.

(52) Ditto.

(53) Ditto.

(54) HIGHEST Order of 27 February 1797, and HIGHEST confirmed personnel tables for Artillery battalions, 12 March 1798.

(55) HIGHEST Orders and Chronicle of the Russian Imperial Army, compiled by Prince Dolgorukii.

(56) HIGHEST Order of 27 February 1797, and Chronicle of the Russian Imperial Army, compiled by Prince Dolgorukii.

(57) HIGHEST Order of 27 February 1797.

(58) HIGHEST confirmed personnel tables for Field and Regimental Artillery, 12 March 1798.

(59) HIGHEST Order.

(60) HIGHEST Order.

(61) PSZ, Vol. XLIII, Part I, Sect. One, pg. 62.

(62) PSZ, Vol. XXIV, № 17,570, pg. 10, and Chronicle of the Russian Imperial Army, compiled by Prince Dolgorukii.

(63) PSZ, Vol. XXIV, № 17,575, pg. 12, and Chronicle of Garrison regiments and battalions, kept in the archive of the War Ministry's Inspection Department, sheet 8.

(64) Chronicle of the Russian Imperial Army, compiled by Prince Dolgorukii, and PSZ, Vol. XXIV, № 17,581, pg. 13.

(65) HIGHEST Order.

(66) PSZ, Vol. XLIII, Part I, Sect. One, pg. 2.

(67) PSZ, Vol. XXIV, № 17,720, pg. 270; HIGHEST Order; Chronicle of the Russian Imperial Army, compiled by Prince Dolgorukii, and Chronicle of garrisons referenced above in Note 63.

(68) PSZ, Vol. XXIV, № 17,718, pg. 270.

(69) Historical Journal of this battalion, submitted to the War Collegium in 1799, and Chronicle of the Russian Imperial Army, compiled by Prince Dolgorukii.

(70) PSZ, Vol. XXXIII, pg. 974, № 26,389, and List of forces for 1816.

(71) HIGHEST Order.

(72) HIGHEST Order.

(73) Chronicle of garrisons, referenced in Note 63, sheet 21.

(74) HIGHEST Order and Chronicle of garrisons, referenced in Note 63, sheets 7 and 11.

(75) PSZ, Vol. XXIV, № 18,308, pg. 9 et seq., and Chronicle of garrisons, referenced in Note 63.

(76) The same Chronicle, sheets 4 and 2.

(77) Ibid., sheet 24.

(78) Ibid., sheet 24.

(79) Ibid., sheet 13.

(80) Ibid., sheet 4.

(81) Ibid., sheets 1-25, and HIGHEST Orders.

(82) Ditto.

(83) In a HIGHEST Order of 4 March 1800, Graf de Castro-Lacerdo's Regiment is prescribed to consist of the

garrisons of Gr. de Castro-Lacerdo (in Reval), Theisen (in Baltic Port), and Tarbeev (in Arensburg), but in the Chronicle of garrisons-referenced in Note 63-sheet 1 shows that Theisen's Garrison Regiment was disbanded on 4 March 1800 and its personnel assigned to Gr. de Castro-Lacerdo's Regiment.

(84) Chronicle of garrisons, referenced in Note 63, sheet 23.

(85) The same Chronicle, sheets 1-25, and reports from the garrisons in Kronstadt and Corfu.

(86) HIGHEST Order.

(87) HIGHEST Order and Chronicle of the Russian Imperial Army, compiled by Prince Dolgorukii.

(88) HIGHEST Orders and Chronicle of the Russian Imperial Army, compiled by Prince Dolgorukii.

(89) Ditto.

(90) Ditto.

(91) Ditto.

(92) Ditto.

(93) Ditto.

(94) HIGHEST confirmed authorization table for this battalion, 29 June 1799, and Chronicle of the Russian Imperial Army, compiled by Prince Dolgorukii.

(95) HIGHEST Orders from March 1800, and Historical Journals of the L.-Gds. Preobrazhenskii, Semenovskii, and Izmailovskii Regiments.

(96) Historical Journal of the L.-Gds. Jäger Regiment.

(97) HIGHEST Order.

(98) Historical Journals of these regiments.

(99) HIGHEST Orders and Chronicle of the Russian Imperial Army, compiled by Prince Dolgorukii.

(100) Ditto.

(101) Ditto.

(102) Ditto.

(103) Ditto.

(104) Ditto.

(105) Ditto.

(106) Ditto.

(107) Ditto.

(108) Ditto.

(109) Ditto.

(110) Ditto.

(111) Ditto.

(112) Ditto.

(113) HIGHEST Order.

(114) HIGHEST Order.

(115) HIGHEST Order.

(116) HIGHEST Order. (117) HIGHEST Order.

(118) HIGHEST Order.

(119) HIGHEST Order and Chronicle of the Russian Imperial Army, compiled by Prince Dolgorukii.

(120) HIGHEST confirmed authorization table for the L.-Gds. Artillery Battalion, 10 July 1798.

(121) HIGHEST Order.

(122) HIGHEST Order.

(123) PSZ, Vol. XLIII, Part I, Sect. One, №17,146, pg. 10.

(124) Order of the Chief Director of the Army Cadet Corps.

(125) PSZ, Vol. XXIV, №18,159, pg. 743.

(126) Information received from the Paul Cadet Corps (Pavlovskii Kadetskii Korpus).

(127) PSZ, Vol. XXIV, №18,793, pg. 488, et seq.

(128) HIGHEST Orders.
(129) HIGHEST Orders.
(130) PSZ, Vol. XXIV, №17,673, pg. 247.
(131) Ibid., №17,903, pg. 523.
(132) HIGHEST Order.
(133) PSZ, Vol. XXV, №18,380, pg. 294.
(134) HIGHEST Orders and Chronicle of the Russian Imperial Army, compiled by Prince Dolgorukii.
(135) Ditto.
(136) Ditto.
(137) PSZ, Vol. XXIV, №17,656, pg. 243.
(138) Ibid., №17,774, pg. 312.
(139) HIGHEST confirmed authorization table for the Greek Infantry Battalion, 13 April 1797.
(140) PSZ, Vol. XXIV, №17,967, pg. 614.
(141) Ibid., №18,227, pg. 785.
(142) HIGHEST Orders and Chronicle of the Russian Imperial Army, compiled by Prince Dolgorukii.
(143) Ditto.
(144) HIGHEST Order.
(145) PSZ, Vol. XXIV, №17,566, pg. 8.
(146) Ibid., №18,283, pg. 851.
(147) PSZ, Vol. XLIII, Part I, Sect. One, pgs. 72 and 7.
(148) PSZ, Vol. XXIV, №17,676, pg. 249.
(149) PSZ, Vol. XLIII, Part I, Sect. One, №17,810, pg. 14.
(150) PSZ, Vol. XLIV, Part II, Sect. Four, №17,987, pg. 301.
(151) Chronicle of garrisons referenced in Note 63, sheet 8, for the entry for the Schlüsselburg Garrison.
(152) PSZ, Vol. XLIII, Part I, Sect. One, №18,091, pg. 24.
(153) Ibid., №18,232, pg. 26.
(154) Ibid., №18,308, pg. 28.
(155) PSZ, Vol. XLIV, Part II, Sect. Four, №18,491, pg. 317.
(156) PSZ, Vol. XLIII, Part I, Sect. One, №18,893, pg. 69.
(157) PSZ, Vol. XLIV, №18,938, pgs. 327 et seq.
(158) Ibid., №19,189, pg. 351.
(159) HIGHEST Order.
(160) PSZ, Vol. XLIV, pgs. 396 and 397.
(161) Ibid.
(162) Ibid., and Vol. XXIV, №17818, pg. 347.
(163) Ibid., and Vol. XXIV, №17,838, pg. 493.
(164) Ibid.
(165) Ibid., pgs. 405 and 406.
(166) Concluded from the fact that during the reign of EMPEROR ALEXANDER I the commands of non-serving invalids were of the same organization and number as under EMPRESS CATHERINE II.
(167) PSZ, Vol. XXIV, №17,552, pg. 5.

РИСУНКИ

Одежды и Вооруженія

РОССІЙСКИХЪ

ВОЙСКЪ.

PLATES LIST OF ILLUSTRATIONS

944. Company-grade Officer and Musician. Ryazhsk Musketeer Regiment, 1797-1801.

945. Regimental Drummer. Kursk Musketeer Regiment, 1797-1801.

946. Grenadier. Kozlov Musketeer Regiment, 1797-1801.

947. Company-grade Officer and Private. Sevastopol Musketeer Regiment, 1797-1801.

948. Grenadier Non-commissioned Officer. Belevsk Musketeer Regiment, 1797-1801.

949. Grenadier Non-commissioned Officer. Aleksopol Musketeer Regiment, 1797-1801.

950. Grenadier. Schlüsselburg Musketeer Regiment, 1797-1801.

951. Musketeer. Bryansk Musketeer Regiment, 1797-1801.

952. Drummer. Troitsk Musketeer Regiment, 1797-1801.

953. Grenadier Non-commissioned Officer. Ladoga Musketeer Regiment, 1797-1801.

954. Grenadier. Polotsk Musketeer Regiment, 1797-1801.

955. Musician. Archangel Musketeer Regiment, 1797-1801.

956. Company-grade Officer and Grenadiers. Old-Ingermanland Musketeer Reg. 1797-1801.

957. Grenadier Drummer. Novgorod Musketeer Regiment, 1797-1801.

958. Grenadier Drummer. Nizhnii-Novgorod Musketeer Regiment, 1797-1801.

959. Private. Vitebsk Musketeer Regiment, 1797-1801.

960. Grenadiers. Azov and Dnieper Musketeer Regiments, 1797-1801.

961. Field-grade Officer and Musketeer Drummer. Reval Musketeer Regiment, 1797-1801.

962. Company-grade Officer and Grenadier Non-commissioned Officer. Tula Musketeer Regiment, 1797-1801.

963. Musketeer Non-commissioned Officer. Yelets Musketeer Regiment, 1797-1801.

The second part of original volume 7 are in the our 2nd volume (SWU-007 Soldiershop.)

912.

Fusilier. Yekaterinoslav Grenadier Regiment, 1797-1801. (In spring uniform.)

Fusilier. St.-Petersburg Grenadier Regiment, 1797-1801. (In summer uniform.)

Fusiliers. Astrakhan Grenadier Regiment, 1797-1801. (In fall uniform and in greatcoat.)

Fusiliers. Kiev Grenadier Regiment, 1797-1801. (In winter uniform.)

Fusilier caps. Kiev Grenadier Regiment, 1797-1801.

Forage caps. Kiev Grenadier Regiment, 1797-1801.

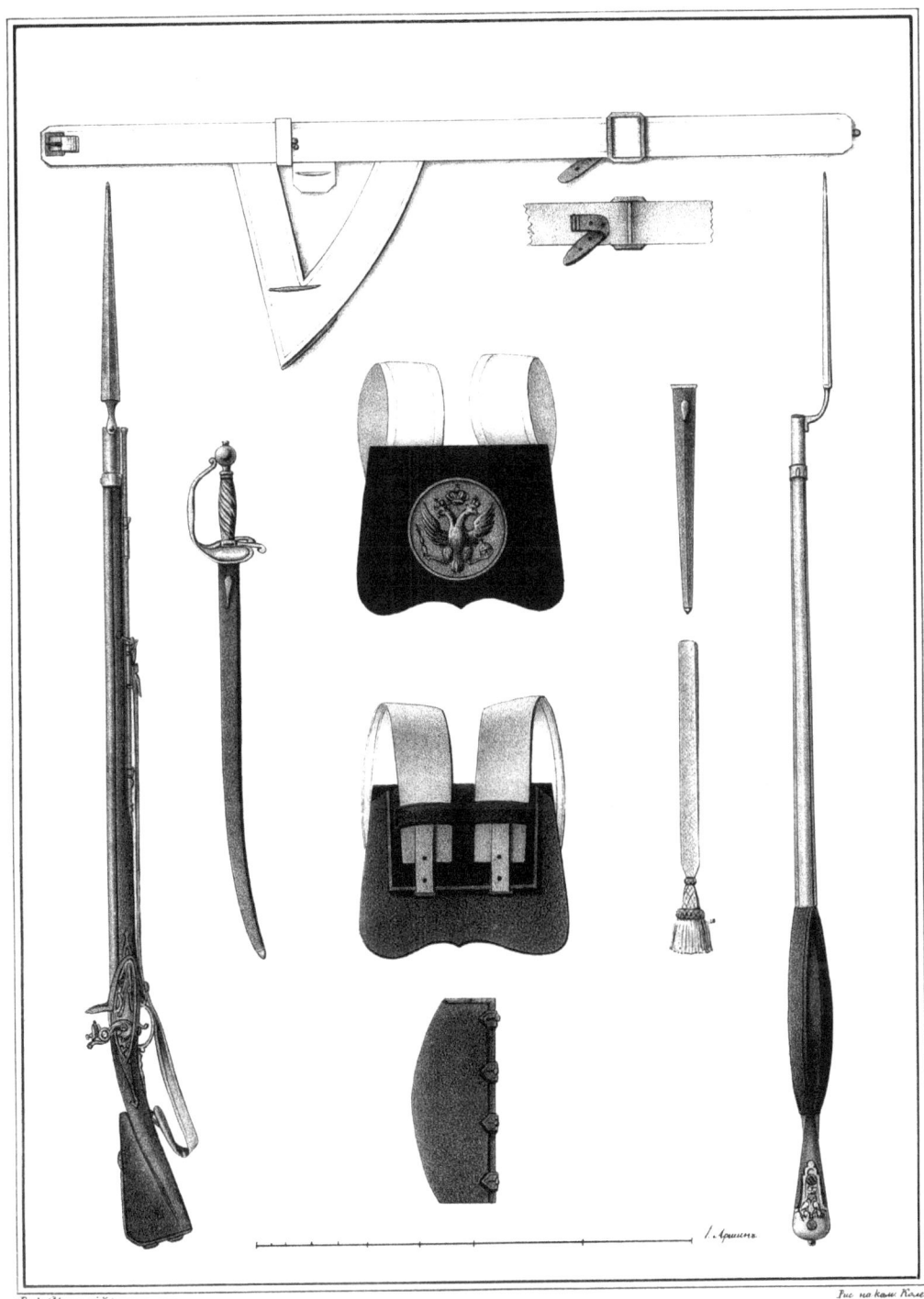

Sword, sword belt, sword knot, musket, bayonet scabbard, lock cover, and cartridge pouch for Privates in Grenadier regiments, 1797-1801.

51

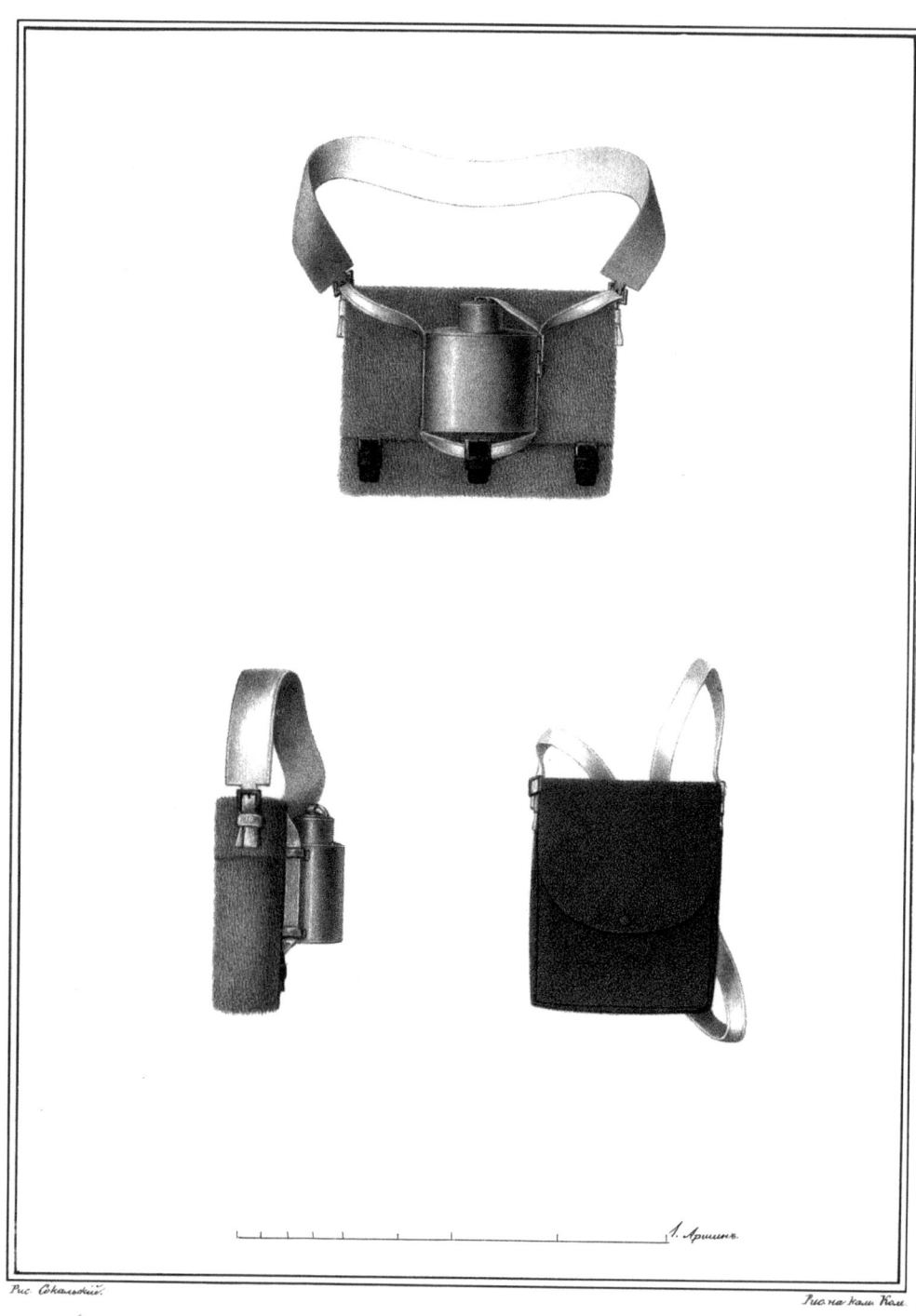

Knapsack, water flask, and rusk bag. Infantry Regiments, 1797-1801.

Non-commissioned Officer and Drummer. Fusilier companies of the
Little-Russian Grenadier Regiment, 1797-1801.

Drum. Little-Russia Grenadier Regiment, 1797-1801.

Grenadier and Grenadier Non-commissioned Officer. Siberia Grenadier Regiment, 1797-1801.

Fifer and Drummer. Phanagoria Grenadier Regiment, 1797-1801.

Company-grade Officer and Regimental Drummer. Kherson Grenadier Regiment, 1797-1801.

Musician. Caucasus Grenadier Regiment, 1797-1801.

Grenadier Non-commissioned Officer and Company-grade Officer. Moscow
Grenadier Regiment, 1797-1801.

Officer Grenadier Regiment, 1797-1801.

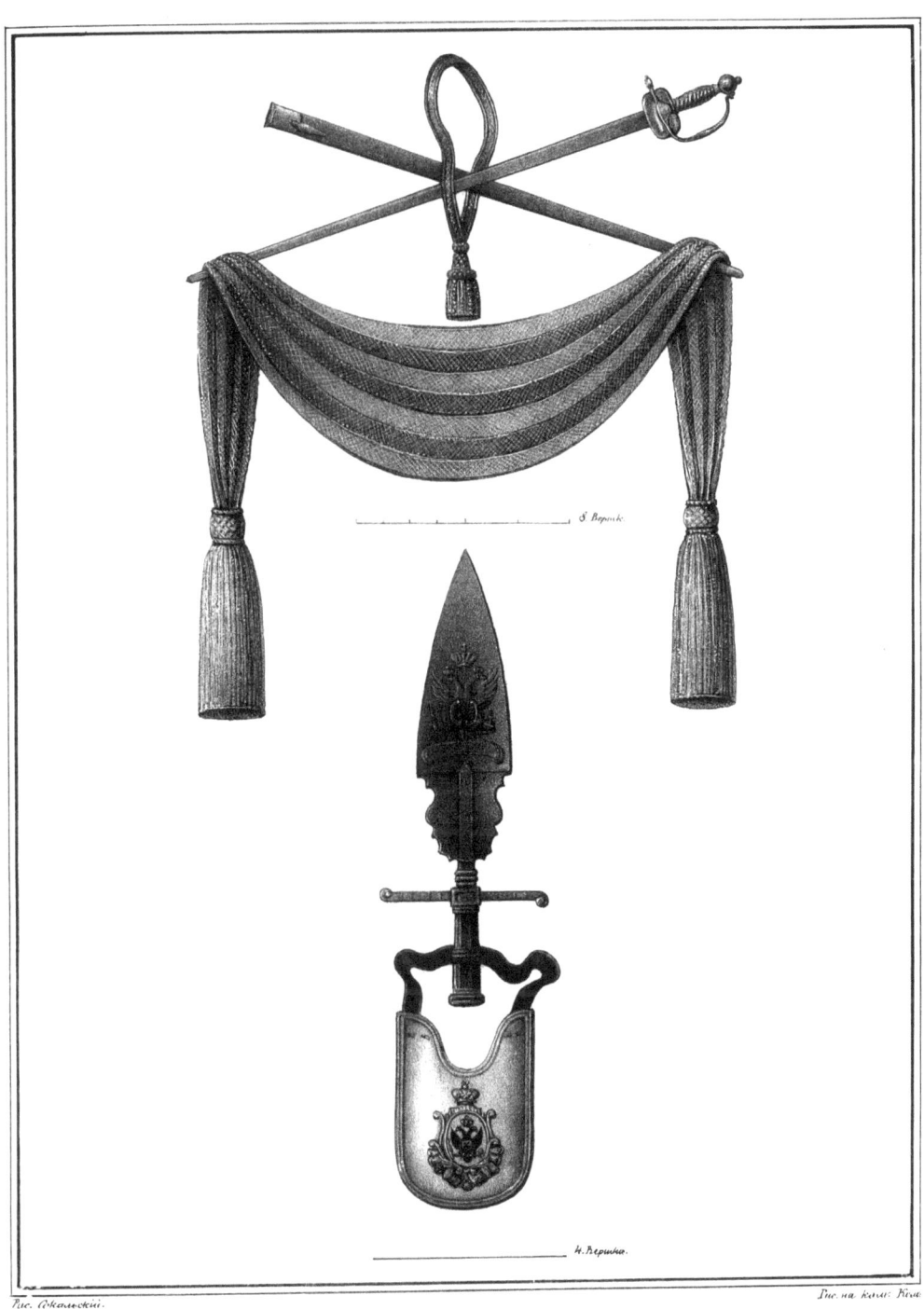

Sword, sword knot, sash, spontoon, and gorget. Infantry officers, 1797-1801.

Adjutant and Fusilier. Taurica Grenadier Regiment, 1797-1801.

Fusilier headdress. Taurica Grenadier Regiment, 1797-1801.

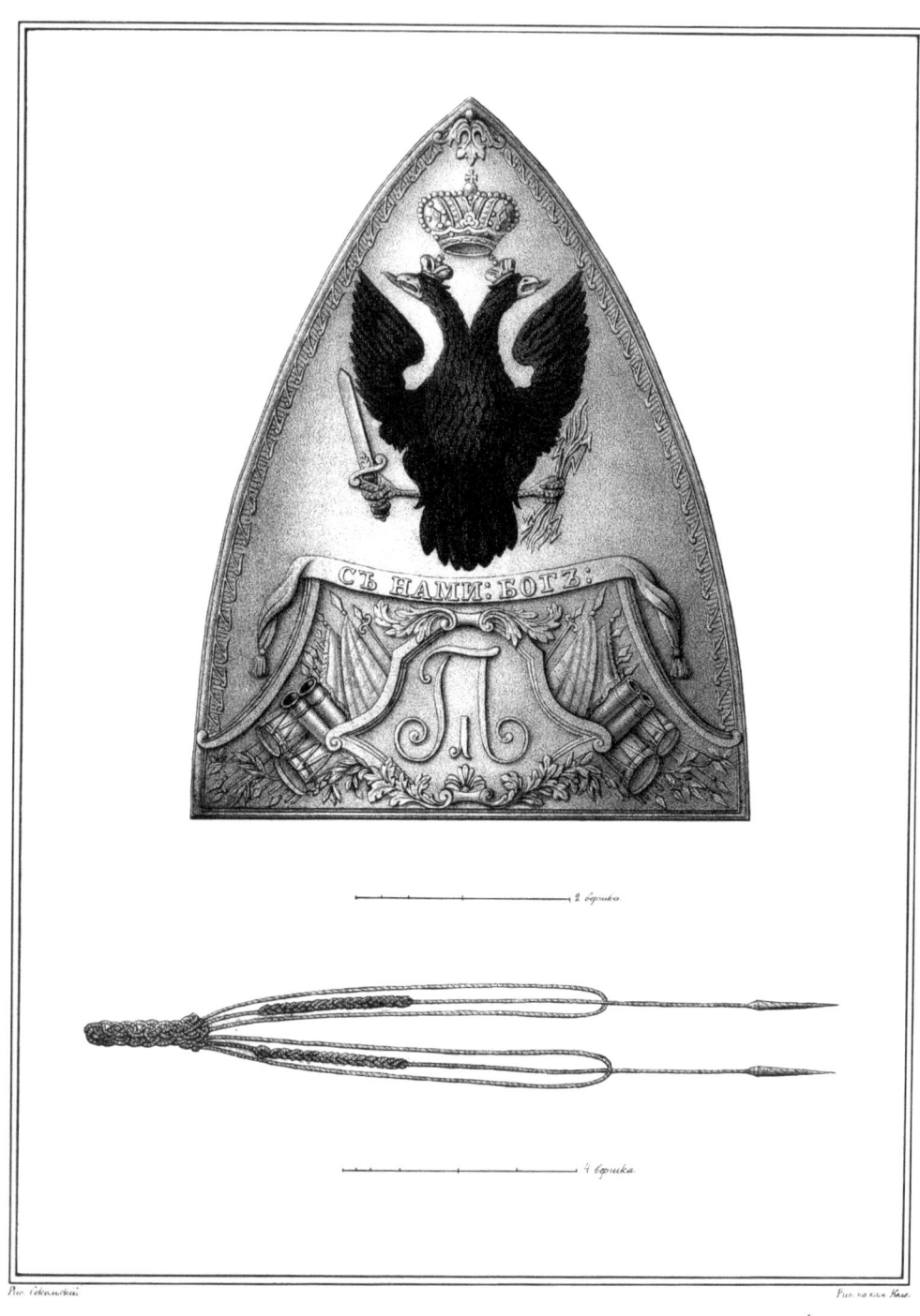

Grenadier-cap plate of the Pavlovsk Grenadier Regiment and Aiguilette of the
Leib-Grenadier Regiment, 1797-1801.

Company-grade Officers and Grenadiers. Leib-Grenadier Reigment, 1797-1801.

934.

Noncombatant. Army regiments, 1797-1801.

Doctor, Auditor, and Quartermaster. Army regiments, 1797-1801.

936.

Wagon Master and Pioneer. Astrakhan Grenadier Regiment, 1798-1801.

Musketeer. Belozersk Musketeer Regiment, 1797-1801.

Grenadier Drummer. Nasheburg Musketeer Regiment, 1797-1801.

Field-grade Officer and Musketeer. Chernigov Musketeer Regiment, 1797-1801.

Grenadier and Company-grade Officer. New-Ingermanland Musketeer Regiment, 1797-1801.

941.

Company-grade Officer and Grenadier Non-commissioned Officer.
Yaroslavl Musketeer Regiment, 1797-1801.

Grenadier Drummer. Apsheron Musketeer Regiment, 1797-1801.

Составл. Василченко и Губаревъ.

Рис. на камнѣ Тиллеръ.

Grenadier. Smolensk Musketeer Regiment, 1797-1801.

944.

Company-grade Officer and Musician. Ryazhsk Musketeer Regiment, 1797-1801.

№ 45.

Составл. Васильченко и Клюквинъ.   Рис. на камнѣ Петровскій.

Regimental Drummer. Kursk Musketeer Regiment, 1797-1801.

Grenadier. Kozlov Musketeer Regiment, 1797-1801.

Company-grade Officer and Private. Sevastopol Musketeer Regiment, 1797-1801.

948.

Grenadier Non-commissioned Officer. Belevsk Musketeer Regiment, 1797-1801.

Grenadier Non-commissioned Officer. Aleksopol Musketeer Regiment, 1797-1801.

Grenadier. Schlüsselburg Musketeer Regiment, 1797-1801.

Musketeer. Bryansk Musketeer Regiment, 1797-1801.

952.

Drummer. Troitsk Musketeer Regiment, 1797-1801.

Grenadier Non-commissioned Officer. Ladoga Musketeer Regiment, 1797-1801.

№54.

Grenadier. Polotsk Musketeer Regiment, 1797-1801.

Musician. Archangel Musketeer Regiment, 1797-1801.

Company-grade Officer and Grenadiers. Old-Ingermanland Musketeer Regiment, 1797-1801.

Grenadier Drummer. Novgorod Musketeer Regiment, 1797-1801.

Grenadier Drummer. Nizhnii-Novgorod Musketeer Regiment, 1797-1801.

Private. Vitebsk Musketeer Regiment, 1797-1801.

Grenadiers. Azov and Dnieper Musketeer Regiments, 1797-1801.

Field-grade Officer and Musketeer Drummer. Reval Musketeer Regiment, 1797-1801.

Company-grade Officer and Grenadier Non-commissioned Officer.
Tula Musketeer Regiment, 1797-1801.

Musketeer Non-commissioned Officer. Yelets Musketeer Regiment, 1797-1801.

WORK PLAN

Our reprint in based on the original 19th century volumes, to be precise the volumes from 7 to 9 are dedicated to the reign of Paul I; this first part is distributed on 7 volumes, having a numbering from 1 to 7. From number 10 to 18 of the original volumes, the second part is dedicated to the Russian troops under Alexander I. These still being worked on and they will be soon ready, distributed on twenty volumes approximately. Our new edition, the first ever published in English, both on paper and digital format, boasts a large number of color plates, many of them unpublished and coloured by our team of expert artists and scholars of uniformology. Each volume is based on 50/70 plates, always accompanied by the original translated text which describes the uniforms, the organization and the armament of the Russian army of the period.

 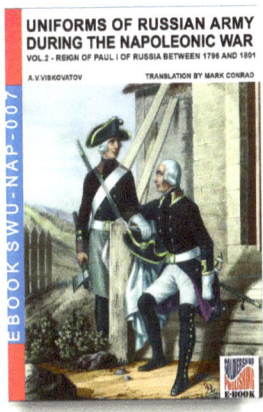